A Gracious Space: Spring Edition

Brave Writer LLC 7723 Tylers Place Blvd. #165
West Chester, OH 45069

Website: www.bravewriter.com

Brave Writer 2015

Author: Julie Bogart
Cover Photography: Tammy Wahl
Typesetting: Sara McAllister

First published in 2015

ISBN-10: 0996242708
ISBN-13: 978-0-9962427-0-7

Contents

Brave Writer

Spring: A Gracious Space

Preface

A Gracious Space is a collection of thoughts and reflections on home education drawn from personal experience and the lives of thousands of Brave Writer families. The spring collection completes the year's trilogy of daily readings. As you wind up your school year, you'll want to finish strong! This volume supports that aspiration and is meant to help you follow through on your best intentions for your family and homeschool.

All of us seek support—whether in the form of in-person cooperatives or online communities. This series of daily readings is drawn from the daily posts I've shared on the Brave Writer Facebook page. This second volume has 50 entries for spring. Pair one per day with a cup of tea or coffee, and remind yourself of your values and your value. Each entry is accompanied by a comment from a parent like you and a daily sustaining thought. As you move through your day, return to the thought and see if you can make it a reality, one day at a time. Progress is the goal, not perfection.

We like to say in Brave Writer that the homeschooling year goes something like this: Fall—Classical Education, Winter—Charlotte Mason, Spring—Unschooling!

That's a little how it can feel—all that strong, orderly intention at the start of the year slips into relaxed, less accountable schoolwork by year's end. Yet spring is wonderful for precisely this reason! As the weather warms up, you'll all want to get outside to take walks, plant seeds, or kick a soccer ball. It's a great time of year to learn to draw or paint, to do those cool science experiments on the back deck, or to take a field trip to the historical sites in your own city. Take advantage of this shift in energy. Don't fight it! It's a gift. You're all ready for a change of pace. Fall will be here soon enough with its sleek objectives and stiff new book spines. Spring offers you a spring in your homeschool's step. Oblige it!

The topics included in this volume cover a range of principles and practices that apply to any homeschooling family. Feel free to read them a day at a time, or in a rush all at once. You might also find these readings useful at homeschool support group meetings. Read an entry as your meeting begins in order to give parents a perspective to consider for discussion or consolation.

The feedback from the parents who've enjoyed volumes Fall and Winter has given me great satisfaction. It's wonderful to hear how homeschooling families like yours are becoming brave enough to have a homeschool that looks just like them! You've nearly made it through another year. Congratulations! Enjoy these last weeks—in bare feet, with cool breezes blowing across your cheeks.

If you need more support on the journey, feel free to check out the homeschool coaching and mentoring program I offer at: http://coachjuliebogart.com. The Homeschool Alliance is designed to give you additional support and help you explore your vision to tailor-make your homeschool.

Enjoy this volume!

Keep going.

Brave Writer

Day 1

Be Interested in Your Child's Thinking

Be more interested in the thinking your child does than the thoughts he or she shares.

For that matter, we might try this approach with the adults in our lives too! When someone shares a strong opinion—even when unsubstantiated by facts and data—it's easy to feel that it is your obligation to enlighten said person with the "truth" —the truth that has eluded them until they happened upon your smarter, more capable mind.

A child is necessarily younger and less experienced with the world than you are, so their opinions will come from a different (more limited) space. But those conclusions and thoughts are no less logical to the child, no less important, no less "true" in his or her mind's eye.

I don't know anyone who has kept every opinion formed at age ten throughout the rest of life. Kids, teens, young adults, heck OLD adults, routinely revise their notions of what is true, right, and good all the time, as they add experiences, information, and relationships to their lives. Our job as parents isn't to "safeguard" a particular set of ideas or beliefs (no matter how much we may hope that our kids will adopt a particular set).

Our job is to value cognitive processes that show our kids are learning to reflect on their thinking. We don't do this to manipulate our kids or anyone else into adopting our way of thinking. We do it to enhance the powers of thought that our kids are exhibiting.

Example.

When Johannah first became interested in animal rights, she wanted to find a way to make a difference. For her, that meant adopting veganism as her lifestyle. It would have been easy to forbid it (since I had to cook for six meat-lovers in the family and her choice would be inconvenient) or to combat it with my experiences (I grew up vegetarian and I "knew" that she wouldn't want to be one forever) or to rebut it with my own set of facts about health.

But what I could see in her commitment wasn't an opinion about animal rights nearly as much as it was an expression of how she "took in" impacting information and then applied it to her life. She was showing me that when she took something seriously, she would make a corresponding choice to back it with her actions! What an amazing development in a young person—to not just rant about ideas, but to put into practice a highly inconvenient lifestyle choice to back up her convictions.

 Brave Writer

As a result, our family accommodated this choice. In fact, two more kids chose to become vegans as a result of watching their sister live out this commitment. We had lots of discussions about how we make commitments and to what causes. It was not easy for my three vegans to understand my choice to not be vegan, for instance. Just my own lifestyle provided them with a chance to learn how to peacefully co-exist with difference—different experiences, thoughts, choices, and facts.

Today, only one of the three is still vegan. They have their new reasons for why they live differently now. These new choices show growth in how they identify nuance in their commitments and what they believe. As I suspected, their ideas morphed and grew just like mine have over a lifetime.

When our kids become passionate about a belief, or when they are exploring ideas that may even seem uncomfortable to us, this is a chance to be supportive of the cognitive development happening right before our eyes! It's a wonderful thing to see a mind choose to think independently of the family culture—to branch out to find information, ideas, and commitments all their own. It doesn't mean our kids will stay with these ideas for good. Lord knows most of us shift identities and beliefs again and again throughout our lives.

Rather, our children, teens, young adults are doing the hard work of becoming—becoming people who know how to think for themselves, using the resources, experiences, and reasoning skills available at that stage in the journey.

All we have to do is buy soy milk, hummus, and Earth Balance margarine, while listening intently to the passionate plea to end violence against animals.

Quote of the day

We have a saying in our house: accept all realities.

Jill Mason Blake

Sustaining thought

Encourage your children's thinking and you will be supporting their growth as thinking individuals.

Brave Writer

Day 2

Be Kind, Be Gentle

I spent too much time today reading accounts of child abuse in homeschooling families. I couldn't stop. It was like watching train wreck after train wreck in slow, horrible, inevitable motion. I didn't want to keep reading; I couldn't stop reading.

The dirty little secret in home education is how much control and anger get directed at our sweet young kids (and awkward fledgling teens) in the name of "helping" them to become self-disciplined models of character and academic achievement. Be warned: A habit of hardness leaves lasting scars.

Certainly plenty of parents are the garden variety that offer big love and abundant support mixed with the occasional exasperated outburst and the daily hand-wringing (sometimes turned lecture) about how to ensure a successful education and smooth transition to adulthood—family jostling and bumping into each other as they make their way through the "we all live together" years.

But some of us bring that little bit extra—that zing, that pop, that overzealous, over-functioning rigidity to our homeschools. We scream, we shame, we blame, we demean, we punish, we prophesy doom, and we herald the end of the world. And sometimes we even succumb to abuse—physical and verbal—in the name of love, in the name of homeschool, in the name of our ideology.

Today I want to say: Shhhhhhhh.

Let it go.

Let your children be children. Let your teens struggle to emerge. Let yourself off the hook.

You don't owe the world a model family. You don't have to get it right. Neither do your kids. Everyone gets better at growing up over time—including you, the parent.

Be the one who stands for kindness in your family. Be remembered for your gentleness. Wait an extra hour before acting and reacting.

Remember the kindness of your parents or significant adult caregiver—the standout memories that helped you through childhood. Be that person for your children. And if you need it: get help. Today's a great day to heal, to start over.

Your kids deserve peace, and so do you.

Quote of the day

"Be remembered for your gentleness." I love that. I never had that person in my childhood, so learning to be that is foreign and difficult.

Heather Winterbottom

Sustaining thought

Your gentleness will be remembered long after homeschooling is over and your children have gone on to live their adult lives.

Day 3

"I Cannot Give What I Do Not Have."

I have one of those calendars with useful thoughts for daily reflection. Today's was a doozy: "I cannot give what I do not have."

My motto is more like, "I will give, give, give, until I do not have, then I will buckle and cave to your pressure, and give again, until I cry."

Home education, parenting, marriage—big hunking depleters! Then the family comes back for that little bit more—and I'm digging through the couch cushions for any spare emotional change.

Daily family life is relentless. No scheduled recess, no breaks—heck no sleep! Yet we're supposed to be:

- Pinterest-level creative,

- unschool-level relaxed and trusting,

- classical-education-level dedicated,

- weekly-therapist-level emotionally healthy, and

- homeschool-mom-level sex kitten (which means you might wash your face and brush your teeth before bed).

 Brave Writer

If it's true that I cannot give what I do not have, what is it that I am giving when I am totally out—spent, done, exhausted, blank, empty?

I thought about that this morning. I'm no longer giving. I'm extorting—I'm taking energy from what would be my own interests and putting it towards the interests of others. Over time, I go into debt to myself and eventually, bankrupt myself (if I don't pay attention).

Bankruptcy looks like breakdowns, the blahs, depression, loss of joy, low energy, fatigue, craving sweets, needing space, resentment, fear, anger, detachment, uncertainty about what I like and don't like.

We owe it to ourselves and our families to pull energy-creators into our lives. It is not selfish, it's not off-topic, it's not a distraction, it's not too time consuming. In fact, if you home educate, you have a moral obligation to keep growing for your own sake. You are your children's primary role model of what it means to be an adult. Your kids need to see you BE an adult in your own right (apart from parenting) so they know to what they aspire. Yes, they will want to parent (most likely), but each of us has a unique contribution to make as an adult outside the family, too.

When you take the time (necessary time—that will not be squeezed in around the edges but will be explored smack dab in the center of your homeschooling day) to be that adult, your kids catch the spirit of adventure that adult life can be!

Meanwhile, *you* expand your brain, refresh your eyes, stimulate your imagination, amaze yourself with your creativity, and use your body for good! You deposit insight, good feeling, pride, optimism, and satisfaction into your emotional bank.

When your kids come running to you with all their needs, you literally have a fat wallet of 'happy' to draw from! You'll be throwing dolla-dolla bills at your kids, because you will feel topped up with energy from your own rich explorations.

You want to know more about knitting? Knit. Even ten minutes a day will change your life.

You miss running? Run. Get a running stroller. Or find a running partner and take turns watching the kids in the playground while you each run a few miles.

You need to expand your brain? Sign up for a MOOC or start grad school one class at a time or read through the classics for yourself.

Your house feels oppressive, tiny, cluttered, and dark? Take it one room at a time and peel wallpaper, paint, add artwork, declutter one drawer per day.

You want time with friends? *Get it*! It is essential to be with other adults. Involve babysitters or spouses and get out of the house, dressing up, laughing, and talking. Even once a quarter is better than nothing.

 © Julie (Bogart) Sweeney | bravewriter.com Brave Writer

You deserve to live your adult life in addition to home educating and spouse-ing. In fact, you must. It's how you stock your emotional tank and your mental resources to help you be all those people who clutter your head with their perfections.

If you are giving what you do not have, go get some.

"Get to give, to get to give." (A wise man once said.)

It's a dance. Learn the steps.

Quote of the day

> *Thank you. I was nearly suicidal before I came to realize that 'self-care' is my #1 responsibility (and not anyone else's job). It is the OPPOSITE of what it feels like: selfish. Without self-care I am not well enough to GIVE to anyone else.*
>
> *Alicia Gurnee*

Sustaining thought

Take care of yourself first so you can give to those you love.

Day 4

Focus on the Child, Not the Project

I want to let you in on the fruit of a lot of late night reading and middle-of-the-night insomnia. The question pawing at me like a nocturnal kitten: What works in parenting? I'm plumb worn out from the sad accounts of kids who are clearly bright, sharp adults who rendered the verdict on their childhoods: thumbs down.

I know that we parents come into the task completely green. Sure, we were parented, but we rarely feel qualified to be parents on that basis alone. We head off to websites and books, retreats and conferences, looking for models that will ensure that *our* children will have good lives and grow up to be responsible, cheerful people. We want guarantees, because life is fraught with chaos and surprises (both welcome and unwelcome).

We trust experts and friends and religious leaders and therapists and anyone who seems authoritative and successful in their own right. We trust methods untested. We hope we are doing right by our kids.

What I am starting to see, though, is this odd trajectory. The kids who claim to have had happy childhoods were not their parents' projects. Rather, the children who grow up to be successful, happy adults are the ones whose projects were absorbing to their parents.

 Brave Writer

See what I did there?

In other words, if you focus more on the stuff that you and your kids care about (the big wide world of learning—books, birds, boats, Beowulf, beauty, bobcats, Broadway, battles, buoyancy, bodies, baked goods, Barbies, Bilbo—and those are just some of the subjects starting with the letter 'B'!), you will create a much more bonded relationship with your children and they will learn how to be competent adults. All the character training you impose, expect, exact, and create through whatever parenting method you choose can never result in the kind of child, and eventual adult, that you and they truly want.

As it turns out, focusing on how to parent your child is less powerful than joining your child in the shared adventure of living. In the end, what leaves the best impression on your kids is your hearty, enthusiastic participation in the stuff of life—and sharing those experiences with them as though they are welcome and a constitutive part of your own experience!

Some of that exploration will be parent led, some of it will be child led, but all of it will be experienced with wide-eyed wonder, a lack of judgment (no more, "Does Minecraft really count?" "Are Barbies dangerous?"), and an investment of the time that really matters, not the time that could go to other stuff like chores, bedtimes, math pages, and baths.

Our homeschools thrive when learning is what we care about more than parenting. Ironically, being a good parent gets tossed into the bargain, when we do. Punishment, teaching responsibility, lectures about character, holding kids accountable to adult standards of behavior—these don't seem to produce the results we think they will.

But jumping into the middle of an adventure—reading, playing a video game, building a bonfire, hiking, calculating to produce a quilt, joining a dance company, visiting the zoo every week, playing with words, baking cookies, acting out scenes from Shakespeare—these do more to "parent" your kids than you realize.

Go forth and be interested in life. Bring your kids along. They'll thank you for it when they get older.

Quote of the day

I've been struggling. This is so perfect. Simple is best. Real life is best. Thank you.

Kelly Rae Nolan Morgenweck

Sustaining thought

Share your interest in life—and spark that interest in your kids—and you'll all be the richer and happier for it.

© Julie (Bogart) Sweeney | bravewriter.com   Brave Writer

Day 5

Once They Catch On, Look Out!

"My kids are getting it!" I'm seeing this theme come through on Facebook, in email, and during phone calls. What are they getting? That what is going on inside (their mind life) deserves a home on paper.

As parents hear their children's thoughts expressed in oral language and help those thoughts get to paper, more and more kids take the risk to cut out the parent-step and try it for themselves.

It's crazy, really. We spend all this time explaining how important writing is, we tell them to follow X model or imitate Aesop or just write three lines, and they show us their sad, uncooperative faces instead. The brilliance of their quirky personalities is hidden behind attempts to sound like someone else. Everyone is demoralized.

Yet if we flip the script—start hearing what our kids are saying in that spontaneous not-school moment, jot down what they say out of our own enthusiasm to preserve the insight, thought, joke, or snatch of story— they perk up.

This is what you wanted me to write? is the thought. You think what I have to say is important enough to write on paper? is the next thought.

Young children, especially, will respond with, "Well in that case" behaviors. They will scratch images and misspelled words onto sheets of paper trying to impress you again! You will be impressed. This child who "didn't know what to write" suddenly has things to say—on paper!

The spelling, punctuation, and capitalization of the words will seem so much less important (and rightly so) when you see the child taking such initiative. Your only task is to fan the flame! Enthuse, supply cool writing utensils, create little booklets (paper folded in half, stapled between a sheet of construction paper), and *read* the results aloud to the child and anyone else in the family who will listen.

The momentum this process creates is entirely different than required writing at a desk every day.

A couple necessary caveats:

1. For reluctant writers who don't trust you (because they feel the weight of pressure coming from you), adopt a bored gaze (this is for parents whose kids get suspicious when they effuse too much). When you hear them expressing, show enthusiasm and jot it down. But when they write on their own, simply acknowledge it matter-of-factly and then ask hours later if you can read it. Ask plainly without over-stating how proud you are so there is room for

 Brave Writer

this child to enthuse or even dislike his own work. Then, when you do read it, praise the content by engaging it—"I love how the princess gets out of trouble" or "I didn't know that about amphibians."

2. Writing programs that teach kids to copy other writers (imitation) sometimes stunt the writing voice. Initially your young writer may look like he or she is imitating a style more than showing his or her natural writing voice. Time will heal this, the more you support and encourage the natural speaking voice to show up on paper by capturing and recording it.

3. Pictures are writing too! Any attempt to symbolize language is writing. So if a child is writing "picture books," without words, affirm the child as writer! As we know, there are loads of wordless books on the market (we find them in libraries). Ask your child to "read" the book back to you. You'll discover so much thought life and language happening in those pictures. As the child gains skill, words will begin to emerge too.

4. Passion for writing comes in bursts. It's a creative activity. A child may write sixteen little books in a month and then nothing for six months. Do not treat writing like an onerous task. Treat it like the creative outlet that it is! You can always gin up more enthusiasm for writing by changing the setting (write somewhere else, use new utensils, add brownies, change the time of day to write).

5. Read what they write during the read aloud time. Put the finished products in the library basket and read them each day. Most kids love this! Those who don't, honor their choice to not be read aloud.

Above all: value what your kids express and get some of it into writing.

Quote of the day

Thank you for sharing! I have found this method to be true with nearly any subject! It is way more fun and inviting.

Heidi Marie Gillihan

Sustaining thought

Discover the writer within your child and his or her true voice by encouraging self-expression on topics of interest and putting those words on paper.

© Julie (Bogart) Sweeney l bravewriter.com
Brave Writer

Day 6

Complexity is Your Friend

A few months back, I interacted with a friend who is childless and has never been married. She's a wonderful person with a number of gifts, not the least of which is her career in banking where she is a skilled, talented, responsible manager of a branch (many people report to her and she does her job quite well). She is smart, a good leader, and a financial wizard. She is also a wonderful auntie and loyal friend.

We got to talking about our families of origin with a couple of my other friends (who had been married or were still, and who had homeschooled their kids). When an issue came up, this unmarried friend gave advice based on her experience of being an auntie and a daughter (both valid sources of information about family relationships, to be sure).

Sometimes her advice felt helpful but sometimes it felt out of tune. I was trying to put my finger on why.

Then she made a remarkable statement: "It always amazes me when someone says that they have changed their ideas about important issues—like how to parent or what they think of marriage or social and political issues.

I've held the same views for as long as I can remember and I don't imagine them ever changing. It seems like people would be much happier if they just stopped re-evaluating their beliefs all the time."

And that's when it hit me. Untested theories about life can remain peacefully intact. If you aren't married, it's easy to have rules about what would end a relationship—until you are in a relationship with children at stake, intertwined incomes, and shared meaningful history. Suddenly your sense of what is a 'deal breaker' can, and often does, change.

If you don't have children of your own, enforcing a set of rules for etiquette, bedtimes, and schoolwork seems so reasonable, so easy to implement. Adults mis-remember their own childhoods all the time. They pretend to themselves that they liked their parents' harsh rules or that they were made better people by the discipline of a school principal, or at the least, that whatever befell them wouldn't have, had the adult authorities in their lives been more stringent or more involved or more kind or whatever.

Likewise, it's not difficult to continue with the same set of basic beliefs about how the world should work, if you haven't had to face the unforeseen consequences of some of those beliefs, nor had them tested in your own life.

I say all this for a reason. This is not you. You do not have the luxury of a simple, satisfying worldview. You are in the murkiest, most-life-testing context of life. When

 Brave Writer

you sign up to be married and to have children, you are volunteering for a mental and emotional overhaul of all you thought you knew to be true. Your theories will now be tested. You will explore ideas and practices you didn't believe in back when you knew everything.

Your need to 'do it right' so nothing bad will happen to you or the people you love, will morph over time as hair-raising circumstances challenge you to reconsider. You'll discover that 'happily ever after' doesn't exist for you (or anyone).

The competing needs for attention, affection, nutrition, and sleep between people sharing a household is of Olympic scale! Everyone goes all in, and there are clear winners and losers in each category every day. You'll be pushed to your limits, which will then force you to figure out how to help everyone take better care of themselves a little bit at a time (including that spouse of yours, and yourself, the last one you usually manage to help).

It's incredible, really, that anyone sharing a home for years on end keeps at it. Really. Truly. Does anyone sync up perfectly in terms of needs? Married couples can hardly get on the same page about sex and finances. Add a couple of kids with high energy, sleep disorders, bedwetting, learning disabilities, and allergies—well, the capacity to match up and have peace is out the window right there.

But here's the magical silver lining to the whole absurd 'Get Everyone on the Same Page' project: you all grow. You grow and you grow and you grow. You have to. It's the requirement of non-monastic life!

You figure out how to get sleep—by sharing and caring and swapping who stays up late and who gets up tomorrow night and how you sleep (co-sleep or using cribs or putting a mattress on the floor in your bedroom for the one scared child who needs you every night). You stop shaming the bed wetter, you take more naps, you require days off, you start exercising and drinking chamomile tea. You keep at it until you get sleep. It might take years, but you work on it every day.

You figure out food—little snack trays, or low shelves with easy to open food stuffs, or six weeks of dinners made and frozen in a freezer, or crock pots, or take out Chinese every Friday night. You handle allergies and learn to cook. You read more books about food than you ever imagined needing to.

You figure out romance—the date night or the one candle that tells the spouse: Yep, I'm open to sexual contact tonight. You swap babysitting with the best friend to have the house alone once in a blue moon, or you read to your honey bear every night before you sleep. You trade flirty texts throughout the day or you take a few months off post-partum so you don't have to negotiate 'Do you want to?' every night.

 Brave Writer

You figure out life—how to survive the overwhelming crushing disappointments that come from failed ideals (friends who betray you; religious communities that stumble; the marriage that can't and shouldn't make it; the illness you didn't plan that robbed you for three years straight; the miscarriages; the house fire; the hurricane; the lost job, lost income, and home repossession; the embarrassment of gaining all that weight due to diabetes, after you had been a dancer in college; the heartache at having hurt your own child; the alcoholism or drug addiction that is destroying someone you love).

In the same ways, you figure out education—one idea at a time, one child at a time, one input at a time. You keep revising your ideas, and then you find new ones that really click. But you know what works and doesn't because you lived each one sincerely. You know your children—you keep letting them teach you about who they are, and that changes how you understand yourself, in addition to them.

Slowly you expand how you operate to accommodate other personality types than your own. You give up notions of phony perfection between parent and child. There is no tactic that ensures a child will match a parent's fantasy of who he or she should be by age 18. There is only love and trying, over and over and over again—until the child knows he or she is loved, and the parent knows that the child is irrefutably a unique worthy person wholly separate from either parent.

Creating a family is the most exasperating, philosophy-destroying, crash-course in love I know about. No two families will get there the same way—but the end goal is a shared one (and a worthy one): to like each other as much as we love each other.

It takes a lifetime.

Complexity is your friend. It will make you into a humble, generous, open-minded, caring, attentive human being—if you let it.

Quote of the day

I have found that parenting, and homeschooling especially, has led to the most personal growth ever (not all of it pleasant, but all of it beneficial).

Stephanie Hoffmann Elms

Sustaining thought

Befriend complexity and it will serve you the rest of your life.

Day 7

You Can Only Do What You Can Do

Every new season seduces parents into believing they can fly. There's something about the start of a new time of year—the blank slate, the brand new, the no-mistakes-made-yet, the intoxicating elixir of 'this season will be different.'

Whatever failed in fall or winter is now up for re-evaluation and redoubling of effort. The urgency to 'get something done' for year-end evaluations, or to satisfy a skeptical spouse, or to appease your own fantasy of what 'should' be happening in your homeschool is surging.

The temptation is great: to completely change gears or programs, or to load up on one particular subject area, or to revamp your schedule so that the one neglected child who was happily playing Minecraft all day is now required to sit at the kitchen table for two hours straight every morning (to prove to you that he is being homeschooled).

My caution: Slow down, Bessie.

You can't change who you are with the snap of your fingers or all the alarms and whistles of your smart phone. No one new curriculum piece will transform your personal style of being or your natural family rhythm. Worse: if you do the 'big overhaul' right now, you may upend all that lovely 'settling in' that would naturally happen in January, the middle of the school year.

Huge shifts in philosophy or practice feel like whiplash to kids. They sense that the changes mean whatever came before was not good enough. (And what if they were reasonably happy doing whatever before? What if they were just getting the hang of the math book or copywork or the system you use to study history?)

It's hard to commit to an experiment, too. Your children aren't reading the home education discussion lists and they aren't necessarily worried about their educations. You worry. That's your job.

So what should you do if you are dissatisfied with the program or the schedule or the feel of your homeschool at this point in the year?

Pause. Take notes. Let yourself consider the good of what is going on in your homeschool before you assume it is all wrong or messed up. I remember one year when I thought we weren't doing enough dictation. I had some fantasy that we'd do it a couple times per week per child.

In January, I pulled out our notebooks where I collected their work. Page after page of dictation. It wound up being that each child (the three who were writing) had practiced dictation 2-3 times per month already, and that meant they had done dictation practice 8-10 times. These dictations, in the shiny clear page protectors, showed remarkable

 Brave Writer

effort and growth. Did they need more dictation than that? The answer turned out to be "No."

But the temptation to revamp the schedule was so strong, I almost revamped without that backward glance. It was a fluke that led me to examine the notebooks and to recognize that with my personality and our busy lives, getting to some form of dictation 2-3 times a month was not only pretty good, it was getting the job done!

This is what I want you to consider. It may actually be true that the practices in place from fall are enough and are a true reflection of who you are, already. It's good to pause, to look through workbooks, to flip through photos, to remind yourself of all the ways you explored learning and the world in the fall.

To make an adjustment, follow this plan to help you and your kids make authentic reasonable changes.

- **Change one egregious subject only.** Don't get swept up into the 'change it all' plan. Save that for summer, when you have time to really think through how the new philosophy will work. If the subject getting you down is your awful co-op composition class for 5th grade, drop it. If your daughter despises the Wordly Wise workbook, shred it. If the math text is confusing even to you, a full grown adult, replace it. Overhaul the one truly awful component in your homeschool.

- **Make logistical changes first.** Rather than throw in the towel on dictation, try new tools or a new environment to see if those recast the practice. You might move dictation to a new time of day, or add candles, or brownies, or use a digital recorder and let the child do dictation alone in his bedroom, or try typing dictation rather than handwriting, or let the child select her own passage, or have the children pair up to do dictation of jokes with each other, or use gel pens and black lined paper. The point is that sometimes the practice is fine, but the context is tedious or unhelpful.

- **Re-evaluate pace.** Does the child need to work every single math problem if she already understands the concept? Can you skip the odds or a full chapter? Perhaps you've been over-doing it on freewriting. Time to take a break and only have experiences, read books, and play with poetry before freewriting again. If you are trapped in Ancient Greece in history (kids are into it and you are sick of it), consider ways to re-hook your interest to accommodate theirs. You don't have to follow the four-year history cycle just because a book tells you to.

- **Add or take away one regular out-of-the-house trip.** For some families, if you just stayed home one more afternoon or day, you'd find that everything works beautifully. You'd have enough time and space for everything without rushing or hurrying or interrupting the flow. But there are some families who are home so much, the kids are utterly bored of the four walls and need an exit! Add one exciting outing a week (even going to the mall, the park, a coffee shop, the zoo, McDonald's PlayPlace, a friend's house, the library) to change the vibe of family life, to have something to look forward to!

You can't fly. You can only do what you do a little better than you are doing it now, until it stops feeling better and you tweak it again. Be patient, trust the process, and go do something *amazing* that enlivens *you* (take on a big goal like traveling for a weekend away with girlfriends to see the Chicago Art Institute, or running a half marathon, or going to cooking class, or signing up to get your master's degree online).

You're already doing a better job than you realize.

I know because I know.

Quote of the day

Thanks so much, Julie. I will step back from the cliff of changing everything, and make some little tweaks instead.

Katrina Daniel Fisher

Sustaining thought

Small changes can lead to enlarged learning experiences for you and for your kids.

Day 8

Don't Turn Down Help

Do you wish you didn't have to ask your family for help?

- with the dishes
- taking out the overflowing garbage
- changing the toilet paper tube (why this is difficult, I still don't understand)
- clearing a table
- putting away the dozens of pairs of mismatched shoes strewn through the halls
- moving a wet load of laundry to the dryer and a new load into the washer
- shoveling snow
- unloading groceries
- replenishing the food and water bowls for the dog and cats

And so on...

Let me flip this around on you. What do you do when someone offers to help?

Think about it for a moment. Imagine this setting. You're in the kitchen unloading the dishwasher and

© Julie (Bogart) Sweeney | bravewriter.com Brave Writer

preparing to load it. In a surprising instance of charity and awareness, your teenager who is watching TV says, "Do you need help, Mom?"

What do you say?

Do you tell the teen that yes, you need help, and that he can turn off his favorite program to take over for you at the sink? Do you then walk away leaving him to it while you go get a bubble bath or hop back onto the computer?

Or do you think to yourself, That's so nice that he asked, I'm going to reward him by saying he doesn't have to help me and he can go on watching his program? Some unconscious version of this one—you turn down help because you feel generous when you do.

Another instance: You're folding laundry and the five-year-old wants to help. He or she will offer five-year-old skills. Do you accept that? Or do you send the child away to play so you can get it done correctly and quickly?

Another time: You're making dinner and it's the favorite meal of your 11-year-old daughter. She offers to peel or chop and you send her to set the table. She doesn't particularly want to set the table—she wanted to help by peeling and chopping. You know she will slow you down if she peels and chops so you ask her to do what feels helpful to you: setting the table. She does a poor job with the table and maybe you then feel resentful that she isn't being helpful.

If any of these resonate—take a moment to consider this idea.

When you turn down help (whether you do so out of a desire to be generous, or because you are better at it, or because the offer doesn't match what you thought you needed), you train your family to *not help* you.

In other words—if you want helpers in your family, accept the help they offer with enthusiasm, support them in being helpful by teaching them the skill they want to offer, and if they are capable of doing the task without you, walk away and let them do the whole job so they get to see they were helpful (not merely supervised and scolded). Let them see that you are relaxing and enjoying the help they are giving you.

It's not easy.

It's a reflex to simply take over, move quickly, do what needs to be done, and leave everyone in the status quo space of not helping. Then what happens? Resentment builds. We start believing that no one cares about us, when in fact, we may have trained our roommates to let us do everything for them!

How do you get back to offers of help if you've already extinguished them? You ask for help! You say things like, "Who wants to help me make dinner? I've got sharp knives and electric tools for anyone who wants to hang out in the kitchen with me. I'll set the table while you frappe and slice."

© Julie (Bogart) Sweeney | bravewriter.com   Brave Writer

You ask for help like this: "I'm exhausted. Anyone willing to do the dishes for me tonight? I will be eternally grateful. I just need one hour to unwind in a tub? Anyone? Anyone?"

If no one offers, you do them and keep going and ask again another night. Over time, your vulnerability in needing help will reappear on the radar. Someone (one of your kids) will recognize that he or she can actually make you happy by helping (not make you worried or annoyed). And that child will offer, freely, out of the blue.

People want to be helpful. Sometimes we train them to lose that desire.

We can turn it around.

Principles:

- Never turn down help.

- Always accept the help being offered (don't change the offer to something else).

- Help your helpers be helpful—give them lessons, show them how, appreciate their efforts.

- Get out of the way—competent helpers should be left to help, not hovered over. You should benefit from the help by not being there, doing something else you enjoy.

- Thank them. Not effusively, but genuinely. "Thank you for cleaning up. That was helpful."

Go forth and be helped!

Quote of the day

Tried it tonight. Our meatloaf has many mountains in it but I'm proud of the group effort. Thank you for the good advice.

Ember Kidd Thompson

Sustaining thought

Ask for help and then receive it—on the helper's terms, at the helper's level of ability.

 Brave Writer

Day 9

Five Principle Elements in Great Writing

Ursula Le Guin, American author of novels, children's books, and short stories, identifies five principle elements that are evident in great writing and are naturally cultivated by writers:

1. the patterns of the language—the sounds of words;

2. the patterns of syntax and grammar; the way the words and sentences connect themselves together; the ways their connections interconnect to form the larger units (paragraphs, sections, chapters); hence the movement of the work, its tempo, pace, gait, and shape in time;

3. the patterns of the images: what the words make us or let us see with the mind's eye or sense imaginatively,

4. the patterns of the ideas: what the words and the narration of events make us understand, or use our understanding upon; and

5. the patterns of the feelings: what the words and the narration, by using all the above means, what makes us experience emotionally or spiritually in areas of our being not directly accessible to or expressible in words.

Quote of the day

The creative adult is the child who survived.

Ursula Le Guin

Sustaining thought

Right now, this minute, you are helping your children survive—and thrive.

 © Julie (Bogart) Sweeney | bravewriter.com Brave Writer

Day 10

Remember to Pause

Birthdays catch me off guard every year, as though I don't know they're coming. As though I have never shopped for presents before, or didn't give birth to the five kids whose birthdays matter most to me.

I confess to *just wanting it to get through birthday season* sometimes. The hassle and hustle triggers my guilt, too. Why do I rarely succeed in shopping early enough to avoid two day shipping prices? How could I let my college kids receive presents and cards after the fact? I chastise myself for being the worst mom of kids on their dorm floors.

Some years I've had every gift purchased and shipped in time. Other years, I'm paying the extra fees for one-day shipping. And still others, I've had to box and wrap a receipt, letting the teen know the gift would arrive within a day or two of his or her birthday.

So it was with great curiosity and interest that I listened to a friend share with me a strategy for being in the present moment—something I need to remember to do for myself. Maybe it will be helpful to you too.

She told me that when she finds herself whipped into frenetic energy, or guilt, or anxiety—she deliberately pauses, for a moment. She checks in with her thoughts, her feelings, and her body—to see what's really there, so she's not just operating from a script of past holiday seasons or past expectations.

The *pause.*

I had forgotten about the pause! It helps to re-center myself and ask the basic questions: Where is my mind (what am I thinking about, or obsessing over)? How do I feel (am I churned up? excited? distracted and edgy)? What's going on in my body (clenched jaw—I grind my teeth so a clenched jaw does tell me a lot about how much I'm holding inside: upset stomach, headache, short breath)? Once I've paused to see what's going on with me, I can then accept it and honor it. I don't have to sweep it away or pretend it's not there or overcome it. I can allow myself to embrace that moment, and the next, and the next one too.

From this place of checking in with myself, I can take into account how I'm doing and that helps me make wise choices. Usually when I blow it or lose it, it's because I am checked out. I'm attempting to fill expectations or am moving really fast or have decided that this moment is annoying and I just want to get past it. When I'm in that mindset, I lose the moment and my choices.

Maybe today we can all pause—simply stop long enough to be present to ourselves and to our families in this moment in time.

© Julie (Bogart) Sweeney | bravewriter.com Brave Writer

I paused this morning. I noticed a lot of agitation and urgency inside. A dismissiveness toward the demands of motherhood. A resentment brewing. It was time for a run, a cup of tea, and a hot shower. Then I'll rouse Noah out of his well-earned slumber, and we'll get that gift I keep putting off. I want to enjoy my time with him, not rush through it (or even skip it). That's what I discovered when I paused this morning. How about you?

Quote of the day

> *Going through life without pauses (big and small)*
> *would be like writing without punctuation!*
> *Commas, periods, or new paragraphs help us*
> *make sense of things, take a breath, organize, and*
> *to know where one chapter ends and a new one*
> *begins. We need these pauses in our lives as they*
> *unfold as well!*
>
> *Amy Cooper Collier*

Sustaining thought

To pause is to cease what you're doing for a moment, giving yourself an opportunity to *be*.

Day 11

Stealth Attack Learning

Rather than teach, lead. Rather than talk, act. Rather than following the curriculum or opening the book, express what you want your children to know.

The secret of a vibrant homeschool is not in a book. It's you. You are the secret weapon. You don't have to be a good teacher. In fact, it helps if you're not. It's better if you are an enthusiast, someone for whom the feast of ideas is so compelling you sneak time to follow up on the material you read to the kids to get the adult perspective. You are the best home educator when you can't wait to make dinner because that's when you park the kids in front of PBS to watch *Arthur* while you listen to Jane Austen on Audible.

There's no magic here apart from the contagious energy that oozes from your engaged, fascinated mind. This is why home education actually works! It's why you don't need teacher training. Yes, you might learn something about how to impart the mechanics of writing or the formulas of math. Of course! But you don't need to know how to give lectures or prepare worksheets or organize data into incremental chunks to be mastered through quizzes and grades.

 Brave Writer

You get to lead by passionate example.

We wonder why our kids don't jump on the train with us? Usually it's because we take that raw energy for the material we are about to learn with them and turn it into something schoolish. We say things like, "Let me check the lesson plan book" or "Get me the teacher's manual" or "I wonder what X curriculum has us doing today."

When we delegate the work of homeschool to a company, we dilute the natural curiosity and energy with someone else's prescriptive expectations.

But what would happen, say, if you read the manual before bedtime? What if you committed 10-15 minutes a day to simply looking at the material you hoped to cover the next day? If in doing so, you could authentically lead with that material without referring to a program or a schedule or a system, what might occur?

Here's what I mean. It's one thing to open a Brave Writer writing program in front of your kids and say, "We're going to do Project Six which is called Body Art. Come lie on the floor."

It's another entirely to get up from the breakfast table and say to one of your kids: "I'm going to lie on top of this long sheet of butcher paper. Would you mind tracing around my body with this big Sharpie? Thanks."

Once the child has done it, you get the scissors and begin cutting your body out. Your kids are going to wonder what you are doing at some point. In the meantime, you keep going. You clip words from Pottery Barn Catalogs and you glue them to your body-butcher paper.

As you work, you ask for help: "Hand me the glue stick, would you?" and "Do you think the word 'sparkly' describes me?"

Before you know it, someone is going to want to have their body drawn and clipped and words stuck to their elbows and forehead too. This is leading and immersing and playing and learning all rolled into one. Stealth attack style—the same way you taught your kids to kick a soccer ball or play peek-a-boo or decorate a Christmas tree. There was no moment where you said to your eight-year-old: "Now let's see—the planner for childhood says you need to learn how to hold a kite string and it will take six steps."

The quickest way to kill the atmosphere of learning is to suggest that it's time to learn.

What do you do with those pesky skills that require some incremental work? You do the best you can to support a rich atmosphere—you add treats, you rub shoulders, you sit next to your struggling second grader, you give encouragement, you try the process yourself in front of your child, you use calculators, you use Spell Check, you add brownies and candles and nature hikes before or after.

© Julie (Bogart) Sweeney | bravewriter.com   Brave Writer

Life is appealing to everyone. Everyone. Life is learning. Invest in what feels alive and good and sparks curiosity.

If what you want to learn is not on the agenda of your child, *you* go learn it in your off minutes. Read an extra chapter. Check out the adult version of the event from the library or online (book, DVD, podcast). Your appetite need not be held back by an eleven-year-old's boredom with the abolition movement. You are free to read all about the Underground Railroad now—without your child coming along.

Trust me: if you become passionate about the topic, you will naturally talk about it in your children's presence and at some point, they will find it interesting or they will have absorbed it simply by sharing oxygen and square footage with you. Perhaps as teens. Perhaps as college students home on break.

If you're looking for a way to start a new trajectory, stealth lessons are the way to go. Set the table with the materials or stack up the books, after the kids are in bed. Get up and begin, without a word, without explanation or mission or objective or preamble. No one wants to be told "We're going to have fun today." The moment they hear the words, they want to prove you wrong. So simply begin.

If the lesson today is all about homonym confusion in the editing process, resist the temptation to talk about the problem your child is having with homonyms. That's a surefire way to kill any interest in learning about homonyms.

Instead, what if you tried this? Before breakfast, fill a white board with homonyms (as obscure and surprising a set as you can find) and then play a game. Ask everyone to illustrate the meaning of each word on scratch paper with drawings, synonyms, sentences, or definitions. Can they Google? Of course! That's how adults learn everything.

Get back to enthusiasm and creativity. Remind yourself of that tedious classroom where you watched the tick tick tick of the clock desperately waiting for the sentence-in-your-seat to end. That will help you remember to keep it real at home—open, direct, clear, interesting—*home*.

You can do this.

Quote of the day

> *As a newbie to this homeschool thing, this is so helpful. Time to start practicing this.*
>
> *Amanda Millheisler*

Sustaining thought

Start with enthusiasm and the learning will follow.

 Brave Writer

Day 12

The Struggle is Human, not Homeschool

The Pinterest, blog, Facebook, Twitter, and Instagram images of happy, successful, engaged, active homeschooled children are snapshots of when all the effort you put in clicks—for an instant, for that one project, one morning, one outing.

I love looking at those images—bright red polka dot teapots, open books on a checkered tablecloth, shell collections with annotations, three kids tossing handmade paper airplanes, the family hike with the dog on a leash, yummy healthy snacks artistically laid out on plates, even the helter-skelter mess of a long runway of cars and blocks and other obstacles down the hall.

We look at these images and think: "I wish my homeschool looked more like *that*."

But the thing is: that's how most humans feel about any collection of images. If you are single and wishing to be coupled, all the married photos and anniversaries and big group outings of pairs make you utterly miserable.

If you are childless and your entire feed is filled with babies and showers and strollers and the little monkey next to a four-month-old pudgy buster, you're going to think your life is awful and the sun isn't out for you.

If you do have love and children and a home—basics that are craved by a huge number of people who would settle for your messy hallways and uneaten treats and the bickering of sleepy cranky siblings—you will still find ways to separate yourself from the feeling of wholeness by simply narrowing the scope of your search for what is missing in your life.

So you notice the types of cozy, livable homes other parents create that you haven't, or the way someone else's child is 'invested' in learning to play chess or memorizing the constellations unlike your stunted-growth six-year-old boy who only cares about ways to torment his little brother with burping noises and won't stop.

We are bombarded with images of exercising, yummy food, fabulous home styles, married bliss, celebrations, generations of family members smiling for a camera as though they all get along famously. We crave what they sell and forget what they conceal.

We add homeschool images and do the same—wondering how we can get our lives to match those single moments of time. You already have these moments, too. You may or may not take a snapshot, but scattered through your busy, messy, not-quite-what-you-planned

 Brave Writer

days are those golden moments of yummy food, cozy home, invested learning, and love. If you could take photos (and this is why so many people *do* take pictures) of those moments and then scroll through your own feed, you might begin to see that you actually are doing it—living the life you always wanted.

It's just that the life we always wanted comes with mess and hardship and heartache, like every other version of life ever lived. You won't get a pass. There's no special key that will end the challenge of raising children so that it is a seamlessly joyful experience start to finish.

It is stupendously joy-filled! We are compelled to have these offspring no matter how many people tell us it will cost us all our life savings, life points, and good looks. The joy—the single moment snapshot joy—outweighs *all* else.

When you start to wonder if you've got the stamina to keep going, know that you do. You will. What other option is there? Within that certainty that you will keep going (whatever that looks like, however your children are schooled), choose deliberately to be alert to snapshot joy. Be a contributor to the stream of happiness out there that helps others get ideas, and the hope to keep trying. Include snapshots of when it goes hopelessly wrong so we can comfort you or laugh with you or stand with you.

The struggle to feel good about your life is useful to you. It motivates you to keep at it, to want to improve, to care about outcome. This proves to me and everyone else that you are not depressed and are doing it right.

The next step is proof for yourself. Please prove to yourself that you are making a happy life for you and your kids. One snapshot, one moment at a time, even if those moments are a week apart. It all counts! And they all add up to the wonder of your family.

Quote of the day

I was recently reminded of a post I wrote of one of those snapshot moments. It does help to remember them if you can. Every morning is not like this, but when I look, I can see it. Especially now that my kids are teens and I can see all the 'leaps of faith' were worth it.

Stephanie Hoffman Elms

Sustaining thought

Each day has its own particular snapshot of joy. Don't miss it!

Day 13

The Gift of Your Presence

All year long, we move in and out of seasons of gift buying, gift giving, and gift thanking. It's easy to forget to be 'present' with and to your children. It is nearly impossible to remember most presents people bought for you. You might recall the Singer sewing machine for kids that your mom gave you at age nine, or the brand new bicycle, or the pocketknife you longed for. But the vast majority of trendy dolls, toys, sweater vests, art kits, Easter baskets, Halloween candies, Nerf guns, and Lego sets—these are happily enjoyed until they are forgotten or wind up lost in the basement.

What is remembered with the gauzy haze of romance and happiness are the shared traditions—where kids got to do what adults do, and were enjoyed in the process. Mashing the potatoes, rolling out pie crust, creating a center piece, singing holiday songs while cleaning the kitchen, hand-drawing place cards with gold ink pens, hanging lights, carving pumpkins, touch football after turkey in the backyard with all the uncles and aunts and cousins, lounging in each other's laps in front of the TV, trick or treating in the neighborhood, decorating and hunting for eggs, staying up late, sleeping in, hot cross buns and cinnamon rolls, and taking turns bouncing the baby.

Ask your children what 'traditions' they love. You will be surprised that some of the things you've done once (!) are on that list and now you know you'd better put them on the list for this year too.

One of our holiday traditions is to make an apple pie with a top crust made from maple leaf cut outs. I did it once—it became firmly cemented in all future Thanksgivings forever and ever, amen. Everyone wants a turn cutting the leaf shapes. My kids are adults. See what I mean?

Each spring, we decorate eggs. We don't just dip them in dye, we first inscribe our favorite quotes from books and movies, cleverly switching out words to include a pun related to eggs and chickens. "My kingdom for an egg!" and "Eggstra-eggstra, read all about it!" The sayings become more and more creative as the years pass.

Be present. Pause occasionally and appreciate the splendor of family that lives under one roof without the need to fly them in from anywhere. Look at the way the children light up thinking about their favorite foods when your energy flags. Ask for hugs and someone to tell you jokes while you bake and prepare the fun!

Give to get to give to get to give to get. This is how the exchange works.

Be present to yourself, to your family, to your joy every holiday season.

 © Julie (Bogart) Sweeney | bravewriter.com Brave Writer

Quote of the day

We have an advent calendar with little drawers.
Every day, we fill it with things to do together
that day: traditions, playing games, watching
holiday movies, baking cookies, exchanging back
massages, reading together, decorating the tree, etc.
It's almost always about quality time together, and
usually something without cost.

Katrina Williams Samra

Sustaining thought

When it comes right down to it, your *presence* is the best *present* of all.

Day 14

To Resolve or not to Resolve

Though January 1st is the most common day to make resolutions, the truth is we all resolve to become the people we aspire to be when the pressure is great enough to overhaul what isn't working. Strangely, the new year's trend in recent years seems to be 'not to resolve'—to say 'no' to the compulsory diets and new exercise regimens, and to be happy with yourself as you are. This competitive, image-oriented culture is exhausted from the relentless demands. Finally. Good for us!

I've never been adept at resolutions, mostly because by January 3rd I forget what I've resolved. Usually I don't resolve to do anything—except to drink champagne at midnight and hope to be kissed!

Until 2014. That year I unwittingly made a yearlong commitment. My best friend and running partner decided in late December to run every day of the coming year.

Every. Day. Of the *year*.

I did not commit to this goal. However, on January 1st, I ran. And on January 2nd, I laced up my shoes and ran again. By January 5th, I realized that I was not going to

 Brave Writer

let this pixie friend of mine spend a whole year beating me in mileage and bragging rights.

I resolved to run every day of the year out of pride and competitiveness. Because it was such a simple goal (run every day—once every 24 hours—no carrying it over to the next day or make-ups possible!), I knew what I had to do each day— even on the day I got a mild concussion surfing, even when I had to fly on airplanes at 6:00 a.m. and had to run at 3:00 a.m., even when the temperatures were six degrees and snow covered the trails, even when I was tired or sick or tired and sick of running!

I ran and ran and ran. I ran in the rain, in the humidity, in shorts, and in sweaters and down jackets. Every day that I didn't wake up and run first thing, I felt an inner pressure all day long to figure out when I would get that run in (sometimes not until after dark). My family and friends knew they couldn't talk me out of running or say, "Can't you just skip it?" when we were on vacations. And I knew I wouldn't let them. It is so empowering to have a boundary like that! It was this one, immovable goal that governed my life for precisely 365 days. Can you imagine how great it feels to say, "Sorry, I have to do this" and then do it? It's amazing!

Truth is: I loved it, even when I hated it. Which is precisely the reason to have a goal or resolution. There's something about the commitment that carries you over the edge from "Gosh this bed is comfy and warm and so much nicer than the 10°, -15° wind chill factor, and dark skies out there" to "Dang, I'm running! This is awesome! I'm amazing! Look at me go!"

The more the days accumulated, the more pressure I felt to keep going. "How can you quit now?" I'd say to myself. And mean it.

So here I sit a day away from the end of this amazing goal (that has hammered my heels, made me gain about ten pounds, and exhausted me) and I'm already sniffing around for another daily commitment.

I remember in 2007 I took a photo a day for Project 365—just one picture a day to post to a blog! Every day. No make-ups. That is one of the most memorable years of my life. Why? Because I was so busy observing it every minute!

Maybe spring is a nice sneaky time to make a commitment—maybe you can resolve to do one thing every day for a month or for the next two months. What can you commit to that is a daily goal that can't be carried over to the next day or crammed into the too small space of the weekend? What is the one thing you can do until the end of this school year that will not be quenched or squelched by anyone because, hey—you said you'd do it every day?

Practice with a small resolution—yoga for 30 days in a row, getting up ten minutes early every day for a month, reading a chapter out of a book you love every night before bed for two months. See how it feels to commit to one thing every day for a short period of time.

 Brave Writer

Here's to the One Thing Resolution! One thing, every day, for a couple of months.

Quote of the day

I want to work on my drawing skills so I am going to draw or sketch something every day. It can be a small quick 10-minute drawing, or something bigger and longer, but putting pen or pencil to paper every day for 365 days. That is my commitment.

Jennifer Ropers

Sustaining thought

It's not what you resolve to do so much as doing what you resolve.

Day 15

Vehicle or Destination?

Don't confuse the educational vehicle with the academic destination. In other words, it is less important whether you unschool or classically educate. Neither of these is inherently superior to the other. They are vehicles that get you to the end goal on the map—an educated, self-reliant adult.

If you become overly enamored with the sleek lines of the Jaguar when you really need an off-road Suzuki Samurai to get to where you're going, you'll be enormously frustrated when it gets all banged up and scratched.

First, figure out where you want to go (perhaps even just a trailhead with lots of options spinning from it). Then pick a vehicle (or vehicles!) that can get you there. There are no moral absolutes about how, only that you make progress toward the destination in a way that doesn't damage your child, damage your relationship to your child, or prevent your child from getting where he or she wants to go.

Sometimes we are so attached to 'the ride,' we disqualify perfectly good educational vehicles because of pride, a quest for ideological purity, or a vague sense of 'this is

 Brave Writer

how I wished I had learned.' Instead, focus on what your specific child needs in your specific situation.

Quote of the day

My experience has also taught me to not be afraid to change vehicles when circumstances require it.

Ann Herndon Corcoran

Sustaining thought

Choose the vehicle that can best take you to the destination you want to reach.

Day 16

When You Lose Your Cool

I lost my cool during the spring break—when I'm not supposed to. Has that ever happened to you? I snapped. Not just once, but a couple of times since my children have been home from college and work. I don't see myself this way—as a person who will 'snap' and get testy or passive-aggressive when I'm under stress. I see myself in this idealized way—that I have patience and perspective, that I can say what I need directly, without using shame or manipulation to get what I want.

But now the kitchen is turned upside down, and my brand new white dish towels are slowly drying with black tea stains, and I'm behind on my shopping, and there are piles of large adult children's stuff tucked in around the edges of each room because that's what college kids do with their stuff when home for break.

Bam! I get blindsided by my own frustration and let it out! It's not so much that I yell. Not my usual style. Rather, I bound into the room already on edge, aware that I have work to do, unmindful of my hunger pangs, and feeling cold. I see the evidence of a meal just made and the stained new tea towel—and I react. I make declarative statements about who is responsible for 'this

© Julie (Bogart) Sweeney | bravewriter.com   Brave Writer

mess' and blame someone other than myself for the tea towels and then expect everyone to pop up and fix it.

I do, almost, cry. Overreaction! Yet perhaps it is not at all an overreaction. Perhaps that is the reaction that needed to happen hours before when I felt past my limit and worried about how I'd get it all done, before I entered the house and found someone to blame for my pent-up anxiety.

The big kids snapped to, including my son's girlfriend, who also witnessed my meltdown. That's when the guilt hit. I knew I'd been unnecessarily exasperated. Fortunately for me, one of the kids called me on it. He stated calmly and honestly (but with hurt in his voice) that I had crossed a line—had crashed the peaceful atmosphere of the home with my anxiety and had misplaced my accusations.

I hate that. I hate doing that. I hate being in the wrong. I hate that I had to apologize to my kids for that behavior and I didn't even want to! But I know it's a gift—that if I can let go of my pride for a moment, I can stop the madness and start over with everyone. Which is what we did. I apologized, so did he, and we cleaned up the kitchen, and ate food, and turned up the thermostat, and watched TV by the fire.

Spring break is meant to be relaxed—a homey opportunity for family togetherness. Weird how that vision can lead to the very things that undermine the goal: chaos, stress, expectation, and moodiness.

I rebooted last night. I'm glad my kids feel free to tell me when I'm out of line.

Quote of the day

I feel as if you were spying on my house this morning. Glad we are all in this together.

Poppy Howells

Sustaining thought

It's okay to lose your cool and it's even better to acknowledge it and apologize.

© Julie (Bogart) Sweeney | bravewriter.com
Brave Writer

Day 17

You Have *One* Job

It feels like you have dozens of jobs and that you might not be doing any of them well enough. But the truth is: you have one job. If you're doing this one job well, everything else will fall into place.

Pinkie promise swear!

Engage the brain. That's it. Your task, as a home educator, isn't to cram a bunch of information into your kids' heads. It isn't to get them to master detailed facts, formulae, or figures. You don't have to have read the entire western canon by the time they turn 18.

The Internet has changed everything. Schools are not doing their jobs if all they offer our kids is a plethora of facts and methods that are easily located online. At home, we have an opportunity to solve the education crisis, one family (one child) at a time. You know what is causing educators to wring their hands? How to update education to the current technologically drenched world we're in now. Learning needs to be about fostering thinkers.

A thinker is marked by these characteristics:

- curious
- able to pose meaningful questions
- correlates information from one discipline with another
- involves personal experience in academic contexts
- willing to take risks
- collaborative
- postulates "what if...?"
- generates multiple possible solutions (not one right answer)
- observes and narrates own process during investigation
- knows how to approach research
- can identify credible versus non-credible sources
- open to creative solutions
- expands the utility of the information into other arenas
- interdisciplinary approach to any subject
- skillful in current technologies

You can use any old content to work on these, from rocks and geologic formations to Mr. Bingley and vintage dance! The content is no longer the primary goal of education.

Thinking—risky, exploratory, curious, probing thought—is!

What does this look like?

 Brave Writer

What if instead of opening the math book and teaching your child how to divide fractions based on the three-sentence instructions on the colorful page, you put out a variety of objects with knives and scissors and asked your kids to do some dividing?

Perhaps you hand them a pie and tell them you need one-sixth of it on a plate.

Ask them how to go about it. Use the language: one-sixth. Examine the term. Ask them what they think one-sixth means or might be. Ask them for clues in the words themselves. We have the word 'one' and we have a version of the word 'six.' What might that mean? What is our experience of pie? How many ways are there to cut pieces? Should we always make skinny triangles? Are there other ways to cut it up? Are there other situations that called for dividing things into smaller pieces? Can we apply what we know about pizza?

Keep going. Let them make mistakes. Let them solve the problem incorrectly. Have several pies ready to go.

Before you swoop in with the right answers for how to create fractional parts, let them get the feel of the problem and articulate it. Let them explore solutions.

You can even solve problems that are quite mundane: "Toothbrushes are all over the bathroom sink and on the floor. I need problem solvers! Let's figure out the solution."

Get out the white board and go to work. Or put the kids in the bathroom (one or two) and let them discuss how they'll handle it.

You can do the same thing with any subject. Let's look at a historical event: the Civil Rights era. It seems incomprehensible that there was ever a time when black Americans were not equal to white Americans. So let's explore that. Are there groups of people in our world today that make us nervous? (It takes some real courage to have this kind of conversation, but there are possible answers—for women, it could be encountering men at night alone, for kids it could be bullies who leave you out of games in the neighborhood, it could be the people one perceives as 'stealing' the right to homeschool...)

Ask questions about history.

- Have there been other times in the past where groups have discriminated against other groups? Why might they?

- What in any of us wants to be exclusive?

- How did skin color make civil rights an especially thorny problem?

And so on.

The goal here is not to run through information and then to master it, but to create space for exploration of the mind's capacities.

© Julie (Bogart) Sweeney | bravewriter.com   Brave Writer

Information alone is no longer enough. You can find it anywhere and it offers plenty of chances to engage the brain. And if you're already doing that, then you're on the right track.

Quote of the day

Thank you. I needed this. Yesterday I was trying to think of what my desires are in homeschooling and parenting. Right up there in the top three is for my children to be thinkers. It isn't an easy goal. There are no step-by-step formulas. But this helped me to get an idea of the type of environment I need to build to foster thinkers.

Meghann Nickoloff

Sustaining thought

Engaging the brain, not merely stuffing it with information, is the goal of home education.

Day 18

Care Less

I'd like to advocate an attitude not usually associated with teaching. I'm not suggesting you be "careless" in how you teach or lead your young charges. Rather, I suggest you "care less" (two words). Can you lean back, put yourself on a porch swing, and let your feet dangle as you glide back and forth, without a care in the world—while you homeschool?

Can you relax your jaw, lighten your tone, and notice the puffy clouds floating by?

We're so invested in how our kids respond to what we offer them, and how we guide them, that sometimes we jinx the outcome! They stiffen or put up their defenses to avoid having to live up to our expectations.

Think about it: Have you ever felt pressured to like a certain meal someone made for you, or felt you were going to owe such a big show of gratitude for a favor done, you almost wished the person had just not helped you?

This may be your kids! It's tough to know on some intuitive level that "my mom's happiness is contingent on how well I enjoy the lesson, or book, or curricula, or activity, or field trip." The part of us that wants to

© Julie (Bogart) Sweeney | bravewriter.com   Brave Writer

have our own original experience resists and balks at the pressure to make the giving person feel good.

You know what I'm talking about—think of your mother or father-in-law or next door neighbor who stands back waiting to be thanked. How do you feel about the service rendered? A little resentful?

Kids have big emotions. They need room to feel and express. It's never about you—these reactions to books or lessons or strategies for learning. How can it be, really? Who doesn't want to be loved by a parent, to feel the parent's approval?

Yet they resist what we offer them when two things happen.

1. They feel they owe you more than they will get out of it for themselves.
2. They feel nervous that they can't live up to your expectations.

So… care less.

Unschoolers use a term called "strewing." It is the act of strategically placing unattended items in the way of a learner—allowing a child to explore the item or book or movie or game—unattended, independently, privately, without preamble or lesson. This is a way you can care less—get out of the way, allow the activity to unfold unsupervised.

Another way: Do the activity, workbook, lesson, game without the kids, without announcement. Get involved by yourself, in front of them, without a word.

Another way: Ask your child for help—in any arena. Does this sound like a good program to you? If you could be in charge today, what would we be doing?

Another way: Openly judge mistakes and flops with a sense of humor. "That collection of manipulatives must have been created by someone with 12 fingers!"

If the house is filled with tension, try one of these.

Disappear. Go into the other room and read a book or page through a catalog, or make yourself a snack.

Grab a blanket and curl up on the couch and doze.

Head outdoors (put the baby in the backpack). Walk, exercise.

Do not judge a day or week or month gone wrong. Care less. You have tomorrow, tomorrow, and tomorrow. You have plenty of time. Take the time you need, trust the process, and care less about the minutia of today.

 Brave Writer

Quote of the day

Amazing the timing of this. These same types of encouraging thoughts hit my heart last night as I was considering the day. It was a message of ease and rest sent by the One who is our rest.

Kim Huitt

Sustaining thought

Caring less accomplishes more.

Day 19

Compliment One of Your Kids Today

Then make sure you follow up and compliment the other ones individually on the remaining days this week and into next week if you need it! Remind yourself—put "Compliment one child today" on the calendar.

Quality affirmation given in a natural, intentional manner yields great results—trust, openness, self-confidence, and a willingness to take more risks. Affirmation need not only focus on a child's successes, but also a child's fierce engagement with struggle. Here are a few models of friendly feedback you can use to help enhance that parent-child bond.

- You have a powerful voice! I can hear it all the way across a room! That's fabulous.

- You were careful coming through that door with the folding chair. I noticed! Thank you.

- It's hard to nap. Thanks for trying to get to sleep on your own for ten minutes before getting up to ask me when the nap would be over. Let's try ten more, shall we?

© Julie (Bogart) Sweeney | bravewriter.com   Brave Writer

- Wow. When you get deeply involved in your game, you can't even hear me call for lunch. You really know how to focus when you are absorbed.

- I appreciate your offer to help. That's really nice of you.

- You sure know a lot about _____. Must take real concentration to hold onto all those details.

- That smile of yours? It always makes me a little happier. Thank you.

- I can tell you're hurting. It's okay to cry. Strong people cry—it's a way to let go and recover from sadness.

You get to help define how your kids interpret their experiences. You can do that using positive reinforcements of their natural reactions—their attempts to be helpful, or to be heard, or to take care of themselves.

Affirm one of your kids today—look for opportunities to enhance your child's self-understanding.

Quote of the Day

Lovely reminder!

Lynne Bowser Holsapple

Sustaining Thought

Notice and appreciate your kids today—for their successes and their struggles. Get it on the calendar, if you need a reminder to do it!

Day 20

Create Space for Play and Breaks

The temptation when faced with learning challenges is to set up a system to address the problems—a structure that will take the issues seriously and will create benchmarks for measurable progress. This kind of approach feels quite "teacherly" and, therefore, valid. We (worried parents) trust a system that is incrementally organized with practices that promise us good results. We cling to the system and follow it to the letter.

What happens, though, when a child balks? Your son or daughter won't do the practices, hates them, and cries or whines that the work is boring or too difficult?

Tension escalates and the relationship between you and your child is at risk.

Certainly professional help for kids with diagnosed learning disorders can be quite useful. Some materials built from these methodologies may target issues that you didn't even realize were related to the disorder or challenge your child faces. Naturally, incorporating these tactics and practices is loving and right!

Still, I want to caution you here. The temptation to get very serious about problems and to follow the protocols to the letter is powerful for parents. We want to believe that if we "do it right," our children will overcome their disorders or learn to cope with their challenges.

Once we get serious, the space for risk-taking, joy, play, and imagination often go right out the window! We tend to clamp down rather than loosen up. The most effective way to make progress with struggling learners is to enhance the parent-child bond, not merely turn to systems and structure. With trust and affection between you, any process you use can contribute to growth.

That nurturing bond is created between parents and children when the parent understands the child's need for a couple of things.

- Play. Children need to know that you value play, humor, happiness, freedom to explore, jokes, and kinesthetic activity.

- Breaks. Kids will try almost anything, but they need to know that if it is too stressful, they get to quit, take a break, or move away from the process or activity.

Create playful ways to address the issues that are not systematic, first, if you can. Perhaps for handwriting, you might use paintbrushes and buckets of water to write messages on the driveway.

Another idea: What if your child stood behind you and put his hands through to the front of your body as though his hands are yours? Have him open a jar of pickles or try writing his name from that blind position. Perhaps you can swap places and show him how you write from that position.

What if you get him in touch with his body and hands and how to use hands in new ways, first, before the systematic approach?

Can he trace words? Can he trace them better if the two of you hold the same pencil and you move gracefully together over the letters—first you control his hand, then he controls your hand?

We are so quick to think all learning happens on paper, with pen, following a set of assignments.

See if you can get outside of this frame of reference—play, take breaks, build trust.

Good luck!

Quote of the Day

Very timely. Thank you!

Cheyenne Foster Johnson

Sustaining Thought

Support structured learning with play, breaks, and creative exploration of the subject matter.

Brave Writer

Day 21

Don't Judge Your Child's Brain

I get calls occasionally from public school parents who want to use Brave Writer to beef up their kids' skill set in writing, using Brave Writer as an extracurricular tool. We're good with that! We've had loads of traditionally schooled kids in our programs.

One distinct feature of these calls is that the parents are highly aware of their children's standardized test scores, IQ numbers, and grades. The system continually assesses students and gives parents sets of criteria to tell them whether to be proud of their kids or desperately worried about them. All this statistical analysis is unhelpful to the parent-child relationship.

Whether a child scores well or poorly tells us very little about the human being living in the skin of your precious child. Spelling scores tell you nothing about the child's mind life. Computers can be programmed to correct spellings—they can't be programmed to tell stories worth reading.

Your child should never know his or her IQ (and it if were up to me, you shouldn't know the score either). Once you label a child's mind as smart or average or "good enough," you subtly shift your expectations (even if you try not to!). You will be tempted to think that your child either should be performing at a much higher capacity (according to some arbitrary standard of what super-smart means) or that that child should be steered away from rigorous academics due to limited intelligence.

Both of these positions are absurd! Human beings are more than the sum of scores and school practices. Intelligence resides in social skills, empathy, artistic promise, and athletic ability as surely as it does in nailing the reading comprehension portion of a pressurized, fake, standardized test with Scantron bubbles.

An aside: homeschool kids routinely perform less well than expected on reading comprehension tests, to the mystification of their parents who know their kids read more widely and deeply than most of their schooled peers. There's a reason for this. Reading comprehension tests have nearly nothing to do with pondering themes deeply, seeing connections to broader concerns, or extrapolating powerful lessons from the story itself. Reading comprehension tests concern themselves with retaining picky details under pressure. Triple ugh!

The best education you can give your child is one where you value your child's natural strengths as they make themselves known to you. You can't know them through tests. You already know them through life—you know your children! You are home with them all the time. Honor and love the socks off those little rascals!

Brave Writer

When you see a child show generosity, say so!

When your kid scores four times in one soccer match, that's the time you say, "You have incredible athletic skills."

When your son brokers peace among fighting factions of siblings, you thank him for being a peacemaker.

When your daughter creates a system that streamlines the shelf or closet where you keep homeschool tools and books so everyone can find them easily, recognize her superbly organized mind!

If you are worried (a child is "behind" in math, for instance), do not test! You know! Get help. Do not limit your child's chance of success by predetermining that that child is not good at math and better work really hard or she'll never make it to college.

Be positive, believe more in your child's mind than the test-makers, and add brownies. Make a plan, stick to the plan. You are not behind. Your child is not "dumb" or "damaged." Your child is your child with a set of experiences and aptitudes. Your job is to nourish and nurture them.

Every brain has a genius. Pay attention to your child's particular bents and you'll find it. Stop letting school and testing tell you who your child is.

You already know!

Quote of the day

Thank you for your constant encouragement. It means a lot.

Patti Condon Hill

Sustaining thought

You know your child better than anyone. Nourish, don't judge, him or her.

Day 22

Every Child is Brilliant

I tell my friends: Brave Writer kids are all brilliant in some way. I know this is true because their parents tell me so. Their kids are ahead of the curve, or read way above grade level, or have been writing stories since age three, or know more about World War II submarines than their dad, or have been painting detailed accurate portraits since they were five years old.

Even the kids who can't read at 11 or write at 13 are gifted, talented, smart, and creative.

Even those with learning disabilities, ADD, and dyslexia are amazing people with powerful brains.

Even those who fail standardized tests have huge imaginations and untapped stores of intelligence that tests do not measure.

Even the ones reading at college grade level but haven't mastered the times tables are much smarter than I was at that age.

This is what I'm told, every day, all day long. I hear these words at the front end of every parenting report—even the parents that are calling because they are worried (who isn't?) that their child is falling behind or won't be challenged enough or is somehow not living up to his or her enormous potential. I understand this. Who wants to fail cultivating brilliance?

They see what others miss. They are smack dab close up to their children. They refuse to tolerate any message that would detract from the clear genius that is this unique person given to them to raise.

When you talk to parents every day as I do, you start to see patterns. Pretty much every five-year-old can tell a yarn that will last 30 minutes if you pay attention and care to hear it. Imagination is the key feature of early childhood—and these free, unfettered imaginations dwarf the tired, cluttered minds of adults. So yes, genius young children abound. What a treat for us!

Most non-handwriters have big vocabularies (particularly home-educated kids since they are talking with caring, interested adults all day every day) and a storehouse of facts tucked away in their heads. These children master the art of memorizing valuable information because they aren't yet ready to record it on paper or screen, yet want so desperately to share and express what they know. What an ingenious way to grow their mental power!

Artistic kids express their intelligence through color, line, form, and imagery. They often surpass the undeveloped skills of their nonartistic parents

 Brave Writer

and impress these same adults with their accuracy or particular viewpoint. They design, arrange, and enhance all the spaces they live in. Brilliance! Talent!

The prolific writers are praised as ahead of their grade level. Parents worry that they will hinder or thwart their children's natural compulsion to write, and work hard to keep the environment stimulating. So many parents call to say their children are writing such compelling material; they are blown away by the scale and scope of it. Of course! Writing unveils an engaged mind life. The mind life of one's own child is infinitely fascinating. Brings tears to my eyes just remembering this experience of reading my children's unsolicited writing.

So yes, your children are brilliant, smart, intelligent, talented, ahead of grade level in many areas, likely to succeed in subject areas you hated in school, and capable of success with or without traditional education, college, or career planning. Your children will surprise and amaze you forever. (At least, that's what my parents tell me!)

All this to say: If you admire your child that much; if you can find the genius in your child even when he or she struggles, is socially awkward, hates math, or can't handwrite; if you are the one who sees who that child really is—a spark of divinity, a brilliant flash of intelligent humanity in this itty-bitty energetic body, an imaginative force field of exuberance; you can't go wrong.

At the same time, please allow your child the opportunity to be ordinary—the extraordinary ordinary that is the right of your particular young charge. Let your sons and daughters not be good at everything, let them take pleasure in subjects and activities that aren't their strengths but that give them joy. Not all learning has to be struggle. Not all success is measured by mastery. Exploration, dabbling, play, and enjoyment are perfectly valid reasons to engage all sorts of subjects.

Remember: No hurry. No shortcuts. If I could admonish no worry, I'd do that too. But worry is how we parents make our way in the world. So let the worry come along in the sidecar. Just don't give it the wheel.

Give your children the chance to be extraordinary and ordinary, brilliant and bored, fantastic and fatigued.

Your amazing, special, imaginative, talented, brilliant children are a gift, first and foremost. If you can remember to enjoy them (more than worry about them), and keep reflecting back to them how much you value all those little traits that other people don't see, together you'll create a magical (real) life and education.

Here's to children! Aren't they grand?

Brave Writer

Quote of the day

Amen, amen! You put in words what I have always felt and told my own kids!

Julie Marie

Sustaining thought

Acknowledge, appreciate, and enjoy the particular brilliance that is your child.

Day 23

Homeschooling is Emotionally Taxing

No matter how many practices you put into place, no matter how much you let go or unschool or relax, no matter how well you love your children—homeschooling is demanding. It requires a level of daily investment that depletes most people.

You're not alone if you feel that way. You're not necessarily doing something wrong. It's important to get relief and to keep working to expand how you homeschool into ways that rejuvenate and support you, so you don't end up bored, depressed, or moody.

But the feelings of significance and investment that you hold in your heart every day are real and carry a toll. I think it's right and just to acknowledge that.

Knowing that the emotional demands of home education are part of the journey can help. At least it's a good place to start.

Brave Writer

Quote of the day

Homeschooling isn't for the faint-hearted! We've been doing it for almost ten years and I still don't get it right every day. But we somehow get it done anyway!

Shari Carroll Teasl

Sustaining thought

Home education is emotionally taxing, even while ultimately rewarding. This is how it is supposed to feel.

Day 24

Inhabit Your Happiness

A strange thing happened to me this week. Two of my adult kids shared essentially the same thought with me. Liam shared that he appreciates college and that he has to remind himself to "inhabit this happiness" rather than continuing to feel as though he is still working to arrive somewhere happier. He's arrived. Time to be happy.

Then just this morning Johannah talked about how she's considering the truth of the idea that there is no other moment to get to. What we need in order to feel content already exists within us. What prevents us from feeling happiness is our belief that there is some other space to go to before we can allow ourselves the feeling of contentment.

I was struck by the similarity of these ideas. We all have objectives and goals. We all want to see evidence of growth in our children. We look for signs of happiness and beauty in our children.

What if today we simply choose to be glad about where we are? What if it were okay to not know the times tables and to have to do visual processing therapies with the middle child and to skip naps and to make sandwiches for dinner?

 Brave Writer

What if we could exercise the "happy muscle" for a few minutes today? Not gratitude necessarily (though gratitude can be a good place to start). More like this: "I choose to find genuine happiness in a moment today. I'm going to let that moment surprise me. I am hereby on alert for a surprise of happy."

During the darkest year of my life, this is one of the ways I got through each day. I couldn't feel happy, but I chose to stay open to a surprise of happy and then to inhabit it, even for a moment.

Quote of the Day

This is something I wish I could do more often. It is so hard not to think of the mental to-do list of life. This reminder is important for me and very timely. Thank you.

Jo Blake

Sustaining Thought

Be open to a surprise of happy today and then, stay there for a moment.

Day 25

It's a Trap!

Don't stumble into it! Surely you can see it coming a mile away. As you watch the smudgy shape on the horizon become bigger and more real, you have two choices.

To stand there and let that perfectly coiffed, smart, capable homeschooler with the engaged happy learners and the bright smile dim your shine with the enormous shadow she casts . . .

Or:

. . . you can step aside, into your own pool of light, and lift your eyes to the sky—take in its boundless open expanse of reassuring space in which to grow and evolve and become.

You have that choice every day. The perennially eager learners are a fantasy—children are like us. Some days they are engaged and enthusiastic. Some days they are bored and whiny. Some days they are content to simply follow the program, too distracted or tired to commit energy to creativity or imagination. Other days you have so much fun, but when you tuck in your darling dear, he declares that he never has any fun at all.

 © Julie (Bogart) Sweeney | bravewriter.com Brave Writer

You can't control how your children respond to your best efforts and conscientiousness. You can't manage your children into model unschoolers. You can't keep up with your best friend or the fantasy home educator who lives in another state, doing it more skillfully and with ease.

What you can do—what you can do right now today—is to be present to your children, your home, and the life you have. The small moments that accumulate to create the feel and memories of your family are happening all day today.

You can help establish the mood of your family simply through paying attention...

- to a smile directed at you
- to a clutter-free space on a table for lunch or copywork
- to the spontaneous sharing between siblings
- to diligence even if displayed for only five minutes at a time
- to humor and little jokes
- to completion of one subject's demands today (even if all the others fall through the cracks)
- to one line of quality writing in a read-aloud
- to picking a flower from the backyard and putting it in a glass of water
- to eating something yummy
- to snuggling a child
- to explaining a concept and seeing the light go on this time!

More goes right than you appreciate.

Keep a record of what goes right today, and sidestep the visage of model homeschooling. It takes self-will and discipline.

I know for me, I get caught in the snare of comparison when I spend too much time looking at photos of other families. I project my biggest fantasies onto the happy smiles.

As my mom says, "Facebook shows us faces, not lives."

We can't know the lives behind the images. If the stories we conjure in our minds make us feel worse about our own lives, we are literally stepping into the trap and are immediately whipped upside down, hanging by a snared foot, from a tree branch.

Instead, get off the well-trimmed path. Make your own way through the forest and notice what you notice. It's quite possible that if you move away from examining what other people do, and pay more attention to the amazing tenacity of effort you give to your family, you will discover much to be proud of.

I dare you!

 Brave Writer

Quote of the day

Yes, and amen! Do not judge your experience based on someone else's highlight reel. Comparison is the thief of joy.

Gayle Westover

Sustaining thought

More goes right in your day than you realize. Notice it, record it, and embrace it.

Day 26

Mother Tongue

I want to live in a world where the content of written communication is more important than spelling and punctuation.

I want to live in a world where people are generous about typos and the accidental homonym-switcheroo.

I want to write in a world where readers value the risk of self-disclosure that goes into all writing, even blog comments, even Facebook status updates, more than grammatical accuracy.

I want to read in a world where people different from me have access to being published, in their natural writing voices—whether or not they use "prestige English."

I wish for a world where communication of all forms is regarded as self-expression, and the vibrant ever-changing shape of language is appreciated, not judged as good or bad or in need of protection or preservation.

I like language and people and varieties of spellings, and deliberate and accidental misuses of grammar and creative punctuation.

  Brave Writer

I love seeing the explosion of self-expression that is the Internet—the spontaneous need to share, express, and be heard. I love that that hunger overcomes the endless drumbeat for perfectly edited copy.

I am less fond of the pride that stems from "being a grammar snob." But I'm trying to love and understand that impulse, too. After all, I know it takes quite a bit of work to master the prestige form of English, and most people who do so are passionate about language, having been rewarded for that effort.

If there is one soapbox that I still mount occasionally, it is the one that says, "There's no officially right way to say or write anything. There is only custom and convention—and these evolve all the time. In the meantime, please—hear the content before you eviscerate the copy."

Quote of the day

LOVE!

Shala Neufeld

Sustaining thought

It's what your kids have to say—out loud and in writing—that really counts. Editing will come, but not until you hear their minds and hearts.

Day 27

Never Enough

Recently a mom wrote what I consider to be the crux of our home-education neuroses.

We never feel like we are doing enough, yet at the end of each day, we are exhausted from doing too much.

Do you know that feeling?

Utterly crazy-making. We're perennially worried that we're not accomplishing enough toward our children's educations, yet each day is overpowering in its demands on our emotions, time, and mental energy.

This is where you have to rally on behalf of yourself.

If you're exhausted and spent, it's because you've used an extraordinary amount of energy toward managing your home and children with an intention to educate all day!

You can't do more than that!

Can you channel your energies toward more productive uses? Perhaps. Some days, for sure. Some days, no way.

Trust that that effort is working secretly, invisibly, on behalf of your children.

© Julie (Bogart) Sweeney | bravewriter.com   Brave Writer

Trust that your worry is evidence of your profound love and devotion to your children.

Trust that your neuroses will drive you to bettering your homeschool little by little, year by year, and that will be enough.

Trust that one day, you will be at the end and you will know that it is right to be finished. It will be time to do something else.

For now, lean into home education and trust yourself. You are the right person for the job. Your kids are lucky that you're their mother. You bring unique gifts to them. Identify them. Celebrate them. Stop looking at your deficiencies. Blaze a different path—the one that is right for your family.

Your homeschool should look like you and your family—and no one else's.

Trust.

Quote of the day

You have such a profound gift for nurturing other women! You touch the deepest place in my soul, like you are the best friend I've ever had. Thank you!

Katrina Williams Samra

Sustaining thought

Your children are lucky to have you as their home educator. Trust your gifts and your efforts to be enough.

 Brave Writer

Day 28

Payday!

Whenever I share about a great moment in one of my kids' lives, my friend shouts, "Payday!" We were homeschoolers together for years. She has eight kids; I have five. We've had our share of challenges and doubts, like any parent. Home education is unique in how it puts pressure on us, though. We feel every setback more deeply—after all, no one blames the "school system" when our kids are behind. They blame us!

We home educators have a hard time not blaming ourselves, too, when our kids struggle. We assume that it's up to us to handle any challenge. We worry—can't remember that some years are years of struggle for a child who, with a little time and maturity, will figure it out just fine (whatever "it" is)!

Home education doesn't always show the fruit we want to see in a single year or handful of years. Some kids who say they don't like home education discover as adults that in fact, they appreciate having been homeschooled.

Not only that, we don't get paid. Not in money. Not in credible experience for a resume. Not in vacation days or bonuses. We provide this service to our families out of sheer conviction that this form of education—this method—has a shot at providing our children with a preferred environment for learning and family bonding.

Chutzpah out the wazoo!

So, on those days when a child suddenly surprises you with an achievement or a good report out in the world, that's when we get paid.

Your child tests well on the Iowas? Payday!

Your child gets into college? Payday!

Your daughter is chosen to be the lead in a play? Payday!

Your son builds his own computer from scratch? Payday!

Your mother finally reports that she is amazed by your 10-year-old's vocabulary? Payday!

The library selects your child's poem to display on its wall? Payday!

Your son's soccer coach selects him to be team captain because of his maturity? Payday!

The child who would not learn times tables with the math book suddenly knows how to calculate percentages because of online gaming? Payday!

You've worked for three years to help your child learn to read, and now, going on nine years old she finally reads her first book aloud to you? *Payday!!!!*

 © Julie (Bogart) Sweeney | bravewriter.com Brave Writer

Your adult child tells you that his scholarship interview went well in part because he shared about poetry teatimes? Payday!

Your adult daughter uses your methods for appreciating art in a museum with underprivileged kids as a social worker? Payday!

Your kids know how to study when they get to college because they know how to teach themselves anything? Payday!

Your children are bonded to each other and look out for each other as adults because they are close? Payday!

There are dozens of paydays happening all the time. What are yours? How can we help each other to call them out when we see them?

You do get paid. Pay attention. Then, take it to the bank—your emotional bank—and make a big deposit.

You're doing it!

Well done.

Quote of the day

Sometimes it really does pay: when your 17-year-old offers to pay for her own art classes because she has a job (that she loves) and can afford it!

Jo Van Every

Sustaining thought

The next time your kids amaze you, say to yourself, "Payday!"

 Brave Writer

Day 29

You're at Home, Don't Forget

I had a question today about what program I would recommend to a child who has recently come out of school and is dysgraphic and a perfectionist. Of course, my first thought is to scrap programs. This kid needs a zoo pass and Legos!

What to do about writing, though. He is struggling and fears it. Of course! We all avoid those skill areas where we are weakest.

To start changing the narrative around writing in your family, even before you buy *Jot It Down* or *Partnership Writing*, make writing more interesting, more useful, and more fun right now in your homes.

Put Post-It® Notes all over the bedroom door of your child. Fill them with comments about his or her strengths, jokes, silly word pairs, brief memories of their exploits, hints about the fun you will have over spring break, questions of the universe ("Who am I and why am I here?" "What is the sound of one hand clapping?"), aphorisms... You decide. Put these Post-its all over the door after the child is asleep and see when he or she finally notices them. You might leave a stack of Post-its and a pen somewhere nearby. See if the child reciprocates. Some will.

Use lipstick to leave love notes for your kids on the bathroom mirror.

Create a treasure hunt—that rhymes! Send your kids hunting for some treat with clues you design. Then later, ask them to make one for you (on your birthday, or for Mother's Day).

Tape words to items in the house—any words. See who notices first.

Play with refrigerator magnets.

Mail letters to your kids. Text your kids. Chat with your kids on Facebook. Even when you're all sitting in the same room (hilarity will ensue).

Write margin notes in the books they are about to read—like, "This was my favorite part" and "I can't believe she did that, can you?" and "When you get to this section, come talk to me. We must discuss."

Leave notes in a teenager's car with cash: "Here's three bucks for a hamburger. Enjoy!"

Use writing in natural, life-affirming ways. See how it changes the feel of writing in your home.

Go for it! Now! Today! It's far more likely you will grow writers if you use writing naturally and playfully

© Julie (Bogart) Sweeney | bravewriter.com   Brave Writer

than if you tirelessly work on paragraphs. Paragraphs will come, once everyone makes friends with writing.

Quote of the day

LOVE this. May be my favorite 'Word of Encouragement' yet.

Julia Reeb

Sustaining thought

Writing springs from a well that is nourished by creativity and imagination.

Day 30

Be Gentle with Yourself

A Brave Writer mom wrote to say she gets insecure about how she homeschools, despite having successfully graduated three kids. She has four more in the pipeline and feels like she is constantly changing what she does, what her expectations are, and how she measures her success.

Here's what I told her:

"Be gentle with yourself. We all reinvent homeschooling every single year. We get tired, we get bored, we get nervous, we get a kid who doesn't do it the way the last four did, we hear about someone else's bright idea and doubt everything we've ever done. That *is* the nature of homeschooling, as the parent. Lean into it and eat chocolate."

Remember: Your children are growing despite you and because of you. Celebrate the strengths of your home and take your glasses off when you look at your deficiencies. Let them go blurry a bit. You're doing more right than you sometimes realize.

 Brave Writer

Quote of the day

Needed to hear this today. Love the advice to eat chocolate! Absolutely. Vital.

Karen Woolley Stewart

Sustaining thought

Enjoy a piece of chocolate and relax as you let go of the doubts and disappointments and consider all the good you do. You're human, after all.

Day 31

Home not School

Home not school—The "re-upping moment."

Remember when you decided to homeschool? Remember what you felt about "school" as a concept? As a notion? You rejected "school." You said to yourself, "I think I can do a better job, or at least a more loving job, or possibly a more attentive-to-my-child job, at home, than what is available at school."

With that burst of bravery, you stood up to "the Man" and said with your actions, "I can do this!" You swiftly researched education, products, learning styles—a crash course in teaching or facilitating or disciplining or modeling or partnering—whatever method you chose—and marched forward with conviction and uneasy confidence.

The first fledgling steps into homeschooling sometimes mirror school. (What else do you know?) But usually it doesn't take long to see that you can relax—pay attention to a child's interest, not do every page, switch routines mid-week, play with Play-Doh for an entire morning, and so on.

© Julie (Bogart) Sweeney l bravewriter.com   Brave Writer

Somewhere along the way, however, you go through your first bout of wavering confidence.

- She didn't read at seven years of age.
- His handwriting is illegible at ten.
- She can't skip count.
- He isn't writing full paragraphs like his cousins in school.

That moment shakes you. Your brain flips into reverse. Just like a new tired language learner reverts to grunting in her native tongue, you return to the only educational model you understand: school.

You buckle down.

You buy new books.

You enforce a schedule.

You require more work.

You follow traditional strategies.

The life's blood of your cozy home slips from view; apples, rulers, yellow school buses, and workbooks crowd your field of vision.

The net effect?

Not progress.

Not joy.

Not home.

School.

School—with its culture of pressure, evaluation, critique, grading, measuring, comparing, forcing a pace, testing, requiring, and shaming—comes flooding past your front door and right into your living room.

The choice to follow a school model for writing leads to stifled voice and plodding progress. Your child's work may mirror the samples, but it doesn't sing. You may finish the assignments, but none are memorable beyond the feeling of "getting it done."

Is this what you wanted? This plodding replication of school at home?

At some point, you may think to yourself, "I miss cozy. I miss natural. I miss the originality of this family."

To start again—to screw up the courage to make homeschool more about "home" than "school"—requires a second commitment. It's what I like to call the "re-upping moment."

That moment is critical to long-term home education.

My products and online classes are all about reinforcing that re-upping moment. You are supported in paying attention to your child's person, his or her interests, pacing yourself, deep diving into subject areas, less is more, writing that expresses self (imperfectly, a bit

 Brave Writer

like a banging drum initially), doing one invested thing at a time, using your real life as the primary teacher rather than canned curriculum.

You can do this, just like you did when you started. In fact, it takes less courage than the first time. You already know you want to! You remember the feeling of joy and freedom of the initial months and years of home education.

Take heart. Your instincts are good. Be home with your kids. Lead them into short lessons, big juicy conversations, writing voice, curiosity, and interest-led study. Your support and partnership make education a joyful exploration of *life*, not merely subjects for school.

You can do this!

Quote of the day

> *Crying . . . I needed to hear this. I need to celebrate spontaneity more and realize anxiety about writing skills is not helping my relationship with my child. So thanks for the timely reminder. You struck a nerve here.*
>
> *Sandra Gentry*

Sustaining thought

Trust your instincts. Trust your kids. Trust the process. You did it once. You can do it again.

Day 32

It's Okay to Take it Easy

Today's "while you sip your coffee" thought: It's okay to take it easy.

You know that day where everything is going along swimmingly?

This one:

- The older kids are quietly finishing pages of math and handwriting.

- The toddler is happily covered in dress-up clothes.

- The baby is napping.

- The pre-reader is sounding out the words easily, conquering Frog and Toad.

- The right library books for the unit study arrived!

- The most exciting chapter in the read-aloud is next.

- Bodies are healthy and fed. Showers and baths may have been taken in the last week.

- All the machines and various household systems work: cars, AC, dishwasher, washer and dryer, ceiling fans, refrigerator and ice maker, all four computers, the DVR, the TV, your lawn mower, plumbing, and gaming consoles.

 Brave Writer

- No one's fighting. No one's complaining. Maybe dinner is already planned.

- You and your Significant Other are getting along—good conversation, good sex.

Sit in this vision for a moment. The vision of well-being—of the stars, planets, and Cheerios aligned. Can you see it? Feel it?

When it comes, when your life hits that magical moment—what do you do?

Here's what some of us do:

We toss a homemade hand grenade into the center of the living room. We reject our ordinary happiness. Why?

Because some of us are under the impression that things of value only happen when we're working hard.

So, when everyone is happily completing pages, reading, and skip counting, when the home is humming and our relationship is peaceful, some of us experience an involuntary panic.

- This material is too easy. She must not be learning.

- He whipped through that passage too quickly. He must not be challenged.

- This book is fun, so it must not be that educational.

- I better take the car in to be repaired.

- I'm going to ask _____ about why (he or she) doesn't _____ more often.

We move into "anticipate the next crisis" mode. To avoid the surprise attack of the next crisis, we create one—one we can control!

Instead of staying home enjoying this (surely temporary) peace, we take the show on the road—adding the challenge of managing lots of kids out in the world.

Some of us buy brand-new curricula so that everyone is suddenly thrust into the learning curve of "new" rather than enjoying comfy and familiar.

We can't appreciate the joy of mastery—we only esteem struggle to learn the next step/process.

Some of us look around at our friends (in person or online heroes) and decide that what they are doing is better, and judge our happy peace as undisciplined or, conversely, not free enough.

We refuse to allow the feeling of happiness to "settle in," because it might mean we are not being conscientious enough about educating our young.

What if we were to while away the hours without diligence and pain and struggle and effort? Would that mean we were irresponsible parents/partners/home educators?

Time for a sip of coffee.

That peace you hear? That's the sound of your life working. That happy completion of pages, the successful

© Julie (Bogart) Sweeney | bravewriter.com   Brave Writer

reading, the repetition of skills learned and now mastered? That's the sound of education taking root.

No one wants to struggle with a new challenge every day. Some of the joy of learning is getting to use the skills cultivated. It feels great to copy a passage without any struggle whatsoever. It's awesome to rip through a set of math problems, knowing you've got it! You get it! You can bury that page with accurate answers and even show your work.

Kids who find their daily groove and rhythm—knowing what is expected and then being able to live up to that expectation—are happy kids.

Don't wreck it!

Enjoy it! This is the life you are shooting for! Problems will find you again, without you even trying. So for now, celebrate the modest joy of ordinary happiness and success. Let yourself off the hook. It's wonderful if everyone likes the curricula, finds it a bit "too easy," and successfully moves through their work with skill. Even professional athletes repeat the same drills at age 30 that they learned in Little League. Mastery relies on practice and practice is all about repetition of skills, not struggling to learn new ones all the time.

You are doing something profoundly right when you feel that whoosh of peace in your home. Pause to notice. Inhale. Then . . . exhale and smile.

Quote of the day

So much of this ought to be elevated to life, and to our relationships, in general!

Elizabeth Templeton

Sustaining thought

A conversation partner is essential to independent learning.

 Brave Writer

Day 33

Managing Multiples

Grade levels are designed for schools, not home. Children similarly aged (not necessarily similarly skilled) are put into bunches and taught by one teacher, using materials designed for that group.

Home educators typically start their journeys with grade level products. They buy the entire slate of materials for kindergarten or first grade. As the oldest gets older, younger kids slide into the 'k' or first grade position. By the time the oldest is in fifth grade, there may be three or four kids who are school aged, all with individual sets of products not necessarily coordinated in any meaningful way for you, the teacher of multiples!

The question becomes: "How do I teach all these levels simultaneously?"

It's a great question! After all, this is not a one-room schoolhouse where children are sent away from the home to a teacher in a separate building, while a parent at home makes meals, shops, and earns an income.

Rather, homeschooling families live in houses, condos, and apartments. They have more going on than an education. They've got pregnancies to contend with, toddlers and babies, all the necessities of life from food to laundry to dental appointments, and the pressure to figure out how to educate on the fly (very few home educators have any kind of training whatsoever!).

The secret to success is abandoning grade level. Focus on subject area, not grade level.

You want all your kids learning about the same subjects together. They will automatically perform at "grade level" or according to their skill set. You can talk about Native American tribes with kids from pre-k to tenth grade. You can gather all kinds of materials and books and use them together. DVDs, historical fiction, personal accounts from living Native Americans, studying maps, visiting burial grounds or Native American landmarks, making foods, weaving facsimiles of rugs or building replicas of their teepees and dwellings. Every child can participate at some level.

The goal is to create a shared family learning adventure. History and science (even literature) can, to a large extent, be studied collectively as you supply skill-appropriate challenges within that context. At least everyone will be on the same page in terms of vocabulary, story, and focus. When you learn this way, students contribute to each other's educations naturally, in conversation, through sharing their work together.

The 3 Rs (reading, writing, arithmetic) may seem like they are more grade-level bound, but that doesn't mean you have to stretch yourself thin like a taffypull to get them in each day for four or more kids.

Set a time aside for when everyone does copywork. Light candles (one mom literally gives a tea light to each child and they write their name on the candleholder). Tell everyone this is the time for copywork. You might be amazed that the youngest kids sustain a longer attention span when they are writing at the same time as the older ones.

Once a week, kids can pick copywork for each other (knock-knock jokes, or riddles, or favorite passages, or quotes from a popular TV show). Sharing the burden is possible. Maybe the older kids help the younger ones find passages they would enjoy. Perhaps the younger ones can offer to decorate the writing of the older kids with stickers or artwork.

When you work on writing, suggest a project and have everyone contribute to it (a family letter, a collective report—each person adding one page). Conversely, each child can work on producing writing for a family topic (subject area). They will select the kind of writing that matches their skill set, but all will focus on writing about artwork or nature or a response to a Shakespeare play.

You can handle math with one child at a time if you need to teach specific concepts. But even then, it's possible to discuss a math concept with the younger ones that the olders already understand. The older kids can demonstrate it in action or they might be partners during Frisbee-toss skip counting. They can be asked to work with the younger child in secret and then come back to show off to you, the parent.

Reading time ought to be all together when possible (memories get made here!). Start with the read-aloud novel (whole family), followed by silent reading for older kids and reading library picture books for younger ones.

The idea is to do things together—as much as is possible. When a child needs your undivided attention, pick a time that doesn't compete with someone else's similar need. Put your child's name on the calendar with a date and time. Be present. The tendency is to attempt to teach important concepts in the midst of bedlam, and then to wonder why the child isn't making progress.

If you keep the family together for most of the day, you also build momentum. You won't be juggling kids who are restlessly waiting for you to help them. Your morning and afternoon will be productive. Dinnertime will involve talking about the immersion in WW2, rather than each child having a different area of history to discuss and no one to discuss it with!

Home education is about a culture of family learning. Drop your memories of grade level. Focus on shared subject area learning, and group projects when you can.

© Julie (Bogart) Sweeney l bravewriter.com   Brave Writer

Quote of the day

Best advice I've seen yet. Creating a culture of learning and sharing as opposed to fitting everyone into a grade category.

Melissa Guthier

Sustaining thought

Learning as a family, regardless of age and ability, produces shared knowledge and intimate relationships.

Day 34

No Shortcuts

There are no shortcuts to good education—whether you're homeschooling, unschooling, or even supervising a traditional brick and mortar education, you are critical to your children's success.

There are no shortcuts. There shouldn't be.

Study after study proves that involved adults (particularly parents) produce smarter, better-educated kids. The goal isn't independence from you. The goal isn't to make you unnecessary. The goal is singular and true for every educational model: prepare children to be capable adults.

Adult life is an interdependent system of self-reliance and bartering/purchasing services you need. Adults read, learn, attempt, do it themselves, take classes, and then either ask friends for help or hire others to work for them. I don't provide my own medical care—a doctor does it for me. I pay. I do make my own meals and shop for my own food. I know adults who hire chefs or eat pre-packaged foods. Both work. No one is self-sufficient in every area.

 Brave Writer

This notion that kids have to be "independent" is an illusion. Adulthood is about becoming responsible for yourself through knowing your strengths, respecting your limits, evaluating options, and making quality choices.

Parents/adults model the activities of responsible adulthood (or irresponsible adulthood) every day they are with children. The invested, active parents seamlessly participate in their children's educations. They aren't "pushing for independence" as much as they are supporting their children in discovering what it is they need, and then in finding (and sometimes paying for) resources that meet their kids' needs.

A concrete example helps.

Public school students may give the appearance of independence; they go to school, do homework, study for and take tests away from their parents. But they are not independent of adult interaction around the subjects they study. A literature class will include 25-30 students reading the same book with a teacher guiding the discussion, providing context, using literary vocabulary, and issuing instructions for activities that help the students understand the book on multiple levels. The classroom context is designed to facilitate a student's investigation of the topic so that he or she develops a literary vocabulary.

A homeschooled high school student does not have that opportunity to sit with an instructor who has prepared a lesson, to listen to the commentary of peers. The homeschooled high school student has parents. The discussion necessary to grow the mental agility to analyze literature must come from somewhere—must be provided. Short of online classes or co-ops, there is one person who can provide that richer context for learning— the parent.

Unschoolers do this naturally (the good ones). The conversations, interactions, and shared learning opportunities may not be on a calendar, but they are happening. Isolation is not good for education. Even if a student shows the ability to read thoroughly and deeply, a child will not glean the subtle layers or the vocabulary of analysis alone with the book. The child cannot see his or her own limited thinking without a dialogue partner. These are modeled to the student through reading additional materials, online discussion with others who've read, and especially with parents (if possible).

If you can't provide your teen (or any child) with that level of support—being available to help that student make the cognitive connections necessary for development—it's your job to ensure that someone is.

Students can learn a lot online in conversation with other adults and teens (discussion boards, blogs, gaming, MOOCs, Kahn Academy). If you aren't available, turn teens loose to find dialogue partners.

         Brave Writer

Consider rethinking the idea that independence is the highest good for teens. Quality interaction with invested participating adults is the best curricula for high school. The aim? To help teens become well informed, rhetorical thinkers who take increasing responsibility for their own lives.

Quote of the day

> *Thanks for this. I can have some of these 'growing conversations' with my older son, but others are beyond me (simply because I'm not home fulltime). That's why I love the high school Bravewriter courses. Romeo and Juliet was wonderful for my 16-year-old this year!*
>
> *Susan Miller Setiawan*

Sustaining thought

To become a truly independent learner one must first depend on someone who knows more.

Day 35

Provide an Education

Your job—provide an education

Your kids' job—decide what to do with it.

Next year, five years from now, the day your son turns 18—these are not important today. Today is important.

Today's task is to be present to your kids. You can't know how it will all turn out. You can't decide now, for instance, that you are training your child to be an engineer simply because she's great at Legos and math. Just because you think your child has a shot at a scholarship via viola doesn't mean the child ought to play viola.

When we script the future for our children, we miss valuable learning opportunities today. We might focus on ensuring a set of criteria (check boxes of subjects studied) rather than seizing the moment right in front of us.

For instance, one mother shared about a kestrel-nesting box her son and husband built together. The son learned to hook up video cameras to live stream the birds for viewing online. As a result, a member of a birding organization discovered their kestrels and came to their home to "band" the birds!

© Julie (Bogart) Sweeney | bravewriter.com   Brave Writer

Kestrel nest building, live Internet streaming, and banding take real time away from Latin roots or grammar books or the study of ancient Greek political thought. Not only that, just because this son became a mini expert in one aspect of birding doesn't mean he is destined for ornithology as his career choice. The experience of caring about kestrels is quite independent of scope and sequence, college entrance requirements, and grades.

Yet it is inextricably bound up in all the elements of learning—reading, studying, planning, constructing, caring, pondering, mulling things over, making mistakes, correcting mistakes, anticipating, predicting, sharing results, interacting with real organizations that care about the same material (in this case, birds), and the eventual satisfaction of "mastery" or accomplishment. That meta-experience (meta—meaning, the experience as template over the actual activity) of learning is what *is* the education. This child is teaching himself how to learn, he's teaching himself about the power of invested, sustained, self-directed attention in the direction of his interests and innate powers.

What couldn't this boy do next? And who's to say what that will be?

There's no need to telescope and think that the content is what mattered here. In fact, the opposite is true. What happened in this activity is that the child moved one step closer to knowing that when he wants something, he has all the powers within to make it happen.

That's the goal of education. It is not the result of most traditional educations. It *is* the result of many home educations, when we pause to acknowledge and value what is happening in front of our eyes.

That said: my kids never built a single thing we could photograph and frame. It's difficult sometimes to see what's being built.

Maybe your kids are "building" a social network online. Maybe they are "building" a mastery of their favorite book series, having read it 13 times.

Maybe they are "building" muscles and skills for soccer.

Maybe they are playing chess or Wii bowling or Settlers of Catan and within each of those games, they are discovering the power of game strategy, calculated risk, the importance of details, the ability to imagine someone else's perspectives through the possible moves they will make.

Perhaps they use one area of interest as a means to an end in another one (our favorite example: a cookie business to pay for space camp—Jacob did this at ages 11-12). He is not involved in either baking or space now.

What did he learn? That when he wants something, the power lies within him to find the means to make it happen—as he's demonstrated through the steady stream of scholarships and opportunities he's created for himself in his career aim to work in international human rights.

 Brave Writer

The interest of today is tied to tomorrow's next step by virtue of the fact that learning is stored inside a human being. That human being compiles experiences and learning opportunities into the cluster of skills necessary to flourish in the world.

The best way to prepare your child for tomorrow is to care completely about today's happiness and interests. You do that by smiling, asking good questions, requesting permission to participate, and narrating back to the child the skills you see emerging from the investment being made. For instance, "Your dedication to beating that video game level is impressive. You've been steadily focused, willing to try again after repeated defeat, and you kept your cool. Wow."

Learning is not about getting your child to a preferred future. Learning is about your child becoming a person who can choose a future for himself or herself.

Quote of the day

Thank you for these freeing and encouraging ideas. You always have such great insight and articulate things so beautifully!

Ellen Dice

Sustaining thought

You provide the education today that will allow your children to create their own future.

 Brave Writer

Day 36

Strength and Stamina

Kids need two capacities in order to build academic skills: strength and stamina. They need to be strong enough to face challenges without collapsing into a puddle of discouragement. They need stamina—the ability to keep trying and persisting past their natural fatigue.

Instead of measuring your children against a rubric of skills (they should be able to write a five-sentence paragraph without my help by age nine, you might think), measure your child's endurance! If your son or daughter is finding it difficult to write, the solution isn't to wring your hands over the fact that your child isn't at grade level. The solution is to build strength and stamina.

In fact, all of education could be reduced to these two qualities. The mind needs to be able to give focused attention to perplexing problems. Focus, when it is on a brain-stretching activity, is tiring. The mind doesn't show fatigue the same way a muscle does. Yet it collapses when exhausted, by refusing to think new thoughts, by becoming foggy and distractible, and by ignoring useful information.

The mind gives up when it is tired. It wants to take a break and does so by seeking distraction or refusing to process information. The anxious parent, eager to hit skill markers, will push, will blame, will require.

"Just two more problems. You don't have it down yet."

"Don't be lazy. You have to work harder."

"If you don't get this done by dinner, we're going to do two more pages before bed."

These strategies are no more effective than telling an exhausted runner that she has to go two more miles at a faster pace because her last two miles were too slow. It's theater of the absurd!

Reframe how you understand your role in your learner's life. To build stamina, to increase strength— think like a trainer in a gym. The initial strategy is to do small repetitions of the skills needed, in short bursts of all out effort.

A child who finds writing tedious and draining will do better writing two words, taking a break, writing two more words, taking another break, and then two more words. That process may seem unnecessary to you, or you may feel that you could never be disrupted that many times in a row and still complete the sentence being copied. But for a child who gives full focus and intensity to the task, two perfectly handwritten words may exhaust the current store of energy in the brain. To keep going may create conditions for slacking off or doing a half job (sort of like lifting a weight half way).

Taking breaks, building up to more repetitions, shortening the breaks between bursts of effort over time, is more likely to get you and your child where you want to go than requiring more and more output just because some scope and sequence says it must be done!

Ask your child for input:

"Can you handle writing two words now and two more ten minutes later?"

On the next day:

"Shall we try that process again, but add a third pair of words? Want to see how well you can sustain your focused attention?"

And so on. Put strength building and stamina ahead of measuring output and you'll see far more growth.

Quote of the day

Again, you write just what I need exactly when I need to see it. Because I was just wondering how I'm gonna build endurance and motivation into my 13-year-old. Thank you.

Julie Antolick Winters

Sustaining thought

Help your children learn and grow with focused blocks of time and they will build strength and stamina.

Brave Writer

Day 37

Surf the Waves of Uncertainty

Pema Chodron writes:

"Our discomfort arises from all our efforts to put ground under our feet, to realize our dream of constant okayness."

No matter what my worldview has been, no matter how well I work out the right principles (for parenting, the cosmos, home education, self improvement, intimate relationships), I'm repeatedly surprised to find that other factors I haven't considered interrupt my "dream of constant okayness." I want control so badly—I want to be assured of outcomes, to be known as conscientious, faithful, intentional, self-aware, and open. I want to know that those in my circle of influence feel heard, valued, trusted, upheld, and supported.

I put all my energy into living that kind of life—the one that is examined, the one worth living.

And still unexpected waves of confusion, complexity, suffering, and pain find their way to me and my loved ones. Even as I try to make peace with the less than ideal, my peace is assaulted again. Even my attempts to "be okay" with not being okay are foiled.

I can't stay there—even the awareness that it's important to accept life on its own terms is one that comes and goes. I can't pin it down and cling to it either.

If life is like that, how much more is something as uncertain as home education?! We are continually revising our efforts, revisiting old ideas, adopting new ones, testing curricula and philosophies. Even as we find a rhythm, someone gets sick or someone ages out of the wonderful plan or we get bored.

The way forward is acceptance of this fractured lifestyle—the one that never quite gets up and running consistently, predictably, with clear results evident to us when we need them.

One way I help myself is to say: "So this erupted and I'm freaking out. To be expected."

Then I have the full freak out! I don't try to thwart it—I just feel it, completely, right down to spilling all my anxiety on the most willing party in my life. I get to work meeting the demands of this new moment as best I can. I have to remind myself that I've been in a pickle before and have gotten out of it, and that I will again. I also remind myself that no peace is lasting and so here is that moment without peace (which means—huzzah!—that peace will return to overcome this "no peace" place).

The "dream of constant okayness" is the message sold to us in advertising, spirituality, education, and relationships. It's a myth.

 Brave Writer

As Pema concludes, we long for "freedom from struggling against the fundamental ambiguity of being human." Yet in our lived experience, we rarely stay there.

Real life is as unnerving as you experience it to be—which is how it is and is supposed to be. Which is a-okay. Ultimately.

Quote of the day

Huzzah Julie! Huzzah Pema!

Nancy Waters

Sustaining thought

It's good and helpful to let go of our need for everything to be okay all the time.

Day 38

Why We Homeschool

Most of us decide to homeschool because we have a hunch, an inkling if you will, that we might recapture the sheer joy of learning and discovery if we would only keep our kids close and spend our days exploring the world together. The simplicity of this natural nurturing vision hits a snag the first time you hear words like grade level, scope and sequence, and common standards, let alone the monolith of mediocrity: Common Core.

It's not that the ideas expressed in grade level or scope and sequence, or even identifying what ought to be commonly held core aspects of education are inherently "evil." It's that once someone creates a rubric, human beings, with their bent toward achievement, competition, and measurement, hurl themselves headlong at those standards and forget to actually learn along the way.

A deadening of curiosity, natural exploration and discovery, and practice occurs. Application and expansion of the ideas are short-circuited with stamps of approval (A, +, credit, and smiley stickers).

We've turned the corner—no more do children need to become repositories of information, which is everywhere,

 Brave Writer

in millions of forms, accessible to billions of people in thousands of languages. Our educations are supposed to help us know what to do with information—how to creatively make use of it, how to manage and transmit it, how to analyze and evaluate it.

I read a terrific article that resonated so strongly with what I think about education. This line jumped off the page at me since it is the crux of how I envision home education. When we talk about smarts, this is what I mean. The writer is challenging the notion that Common Core is any kind of educational salvation. He goes on to ask what methods will we use that will lead to truly educated children:

> *"Instead of trying to codify information from past centuries, we better be looking at how students will handle the incoming flow of traffic. Or how to stimulate creative design thinking. Or how to make them smart enough—meaning curious, resilient, persistent, empathetic, and open enough—to live and perform in today's world."*

Let me pull those words out:

- curious
- resilient
- persistent
- empathetic
- open

Those can be the most natural by-products of home education. If we can move beyond thinking of content for content's sake, and instead see content as an opportunity to expand those aspects of our children's character and mental agility, we will indeed be giving a rich education to our charges.

This terrific article, written to traditional teachers, is actually better directed to educators at home. After all, you don't have the state breathing down your neck. You have the protection of your four walls and your rights.

So go for it!

The concluding thought ought to reassure you that traditional education is in crisis—what you're doing *is* the future of education.

> *"Untold damage has been done in the last ten years by the relentless focus on dispensing information to students like pills. That approach ignores the deep, magical relationship between purpose, curiosity, and intelligence—the mix that creates 'openness' to learning and makes engagement natural. More of the same won't do anything but dumb us down."* *(Terry Heick)*

Quote of the day

> *Education is not the filling of a pail, but the lighting of a fire.*
>
> *William Butler Yeats*

Sustaining thought

"The most influential of all educational factors is the conversation in a child's home." (William Temple)

Day 39

Your Teenagers' Thoughts are Interesting

. . . even if they are thoughts you have never thought to think! Sometimes a parent will tell me their child doesn't have any interests or passions and that's the problem. It could be that the parents can't detect the interests so they can't support them.

Let's back up. Ask yourself first: "What thoughts is my child having? What does my child think about?" Do you even know?

At least 12 hours of the day, all of us spend energy thinking—about stuff. These thoughts range from regular, "quotidienne" (daily) stuff like, "I'm starved. I wonder when I can eat lunch" to our aspirations "Gawd, I hope she texts me back."

These thoughts take energy and some of them dominate our minds for hours/days at a time. Your teen "without the interests" is thinking during all those hours of the day, just like your teen "with a passion" is. However, the thoughts of the "teen who seems not to have an interest" are invisible to you. That's because you don't know to ask about them. You are looking for

 Brave Writer

evidence of thoughts that you understand, care about, and admire.

If you saw your child playing chess every day, even if you weren't a chess player, your bearing would show pride and approval. You value chess. You think chess proves intelligence. Kids pick this up. They know which of their thoughts are "permitted" to be shared, and which must remain "private."

For instance, if you have a child who is thinking a lot about how to beat the next level of Halo (video game), that pattern of thought is taking up the hours in the day. Halo is the interest. Halo may even be the passion.

For me, a grown woman who never played a video game in her life as a child, Halo is invisible to me. The thoughts about it, the vocabulary that goes with it, the anxieties that attend it, the enthusiasms and achievements that spring from it—I have no way to appreciate, care about, or express curiosity for that world. I mostly ignore it. I literally don't hear the words the child says when he is talking about it. My mind drifts and eventually it never comes up any more.

As a result, this precious child of mine exists in a privately created world. When asked about his passions, he's already picked up that the family culture doesn't see "Halo" as a valid interest or passion so he says he doesn't have any. But it's not true, right? He has an "illegal" interest.

Let me interject a little story. When Liam was in high

school, he was a huge Warcraft fan. He played many hours a day. One day I was working on my computer when he called out to me, "Mom I just got to this really high level. In fact, my team is so good, gamers in Korea are watching us online."

I nodded a vague, "Uh huh. Good Liam"—never raising my eyes.

Then he said more loudly, "*Mom!* Come over here. You don't understand this but I want to show you. This is a really big deal and I need you to get it."

Wow! He was right. I didn't get that I didn't get it until that moment. I went to his computer and for the next hour he explained to me how difficult it was to rise to this level. He showed me his wins and losses, his teammates, and how the game was played and watched halfway around the world.

It was a moment!

It was so easy to approve of kids who were writing college applications and earning scholarships. It was easy to root for kids who were playing lacrosse or soccer. I could applaud wildly when my older kids performed in Shakespeare plays.

Yet here was Liam, brilliant of course, living in a privately-nourished world of skill and community invisible to all of us, unvalued by most of us in the family, but in particular, his mother—me.

 © Julie (Bogart) Sweeney | bravewriter.com Brave Writer

Our job as parents isn't to determine in advance what we want our kids to care about. Our job is to care about our kids—in all their varied complexity. Your kids can learn everything they need to learn about learning through the stuff that fills their minds right now. We have to choose not to filter their lives through our own value set (rendering what they care about invisible to us).

You want your child to care about spelling? Why not be curious about how the gaming community sees spelling? Is it important? What does it say about a gamer when he is typing his thoughts and they are misspelled? Are there games that are known for being crummy games because the writing about the game is poorly edited? Or does it even matter?

You want your child to be a good thinker? Find out how he uses his mind for his interests. Ask: "What is your strategy when you play solo versus when you play on a team? How do you decide who the leader of the team is? Have you taken a turn as leader? Do you want to? Why or why not? Are you ever troubled by the shooting? Why or why not? How do you decide one game is well made and another isn't?"

The goal of education isn't to get your kids to like subjects you consider worthy of attention. The goal of education is to help kids discover how their brains work—so they can use that brain for anything they choose for their lives.

Subject area information is important insofar as it advances a child's ability to function successfully in adult life. We can get there by many means, and the chief one ought to be engaging the active mind life that is already busy and curious no matter what is happening between the ears.

Go forth and be curious about your amazing kids!

Quote of the day

Oh my yes! And when you honor those interests that you don't understand, they get used to sharing their thoughts with you, which makes it easier as they get older for them to continue sharing.

Stephanie Hoffman Elms

Sustaining thought

Curiosity and conversation about your kids' interests lead to intimacy and trust.

Day 40

Conversations in the Car Count

You're driving along discussing how far the sun is from the earth when one of your kids wants to know if the song on the radio is by One Republic. Another one asks if you can stop by the store to get a Star Fruit because she heard about it from a book she's reading, and then another one declares that he knows a shortcut home. The toddler throws his pacifier to the floor and the nine-year-old steps on it while trying to pick it up. Of course.

In the span of fifteen minutes, you've covered all kinds of interesting information, as well as heard snippets of what is filling your kids' heads all day, in addition to the inevitable interruptions of life with children.

Count it all.

Write it down.

It's okay that you have incomplete discussions. You'll circle back to them over time. Remind yourself that conversation is the homeschool equivalent of classroom lecture. These conversations are often best had in a car, anyway. That's when you're all trapped in one space and talking is the main thing you can do in that space.

Use it well! Ask a provocative question: "How many whole chickens could we fit in that semi? How might we figure it out?" Brainstorm ideas, take guesses, and figure it out when you get home.

Ponder other questions: "I wonder how long it would take to ride a horse to the store rather than drive a car." Discuss. You might talk about the pop star or the lyrics of a song. You might comment on the birds on the telephone wire, wondering which kind they are. You might ask about a game recently played or a book being read.

Talk in the car! Count it. So much good education happens, literally, along the way.

Quote of the day

Our best, often deepest, conversations happen in the car. I always 'count' the car when it comes to homeschool record keeping with my 13-year-old.

Sahara Violet Anderson

Sustaining thought

Cozy times, learning times, fun times, errand times— all while riding in a car together. Count them as some of your best with your kids.

Day 41

Forgetfulness

The other day I was helping Liam get ready to leave to work at a summer camp in the Poconos. We were going over all the details of what he needed to remember to bring. Several times he moved one item, and then we'd nearly forget it. But I didn't. I'd neurotically double and triple check to be sure we didn't lose a thing.

He explained that it's hard for him to keep track of stuff, unlike me who never loses anything. Blink, blink. Are you kidding me?

At that point I explained that I gave up playing flute because I lost my flute so many times; that I couldn't keep track of a purse so didn't use one for years; that I've lost multiple pairs of expensive ski glasses; I've gone to a foreign country without a passport and another one without a required Visa.

I've lost film, overlooked critical deadlines for membership societies, missed almost a year's worth of piano lessons for Noah (we'd forget three out of four a month), and have no system for filing documents like birth certificates, wills, social security cards (which happen to be pinned to my bulletin board currently) or taxes.

As a result, I am the teensiest bit neurotic about details when confronted with them, certain that I am forgetting something. Which is why I appear to remember them. And did on Sunday. Go me!

Until I opened Liam's college file (finally, in a moment of quiet) to discover that we had completely forgotten to schedule a physical or update his immunizations before he left—and the deadline is August 1. Of course Liam returns August 16th.

After a sleepless night and many phone calls, an extension was bestowed and we are back in business. But now I know why at age 52 I'm a nutcase and a neurotic perfectionist. It's the only way I can compensate for my natural proclivity to be forgetful. It amazes me that I get anything done!

Quote of the day

> *I can relate to the umpteenth degree. I have lost my passport in a foreign country, have no filing system for birth certificates, etc. and I lose my keys on almost daily basis. Oh, and the kicker? My son is also named Liam.*
>
> *Mary Bristol*

Sustaining thought

Perhaps Khalil Gibran makes a good point! *"Forgetfulness is a form of freedom."*

© Julie (Bogart) Sweeney | bravewriter.com   Brave Writer

Day 42

Give Your Children a Gift

Honor their interpretation of what happened in their lives.

Whether your child is 5, 15, or 25—that individual human being, product of your love, will one day tell you that something you did harmed him or her. It will show up in a five-year-old's "You hurt my feelings" or "You're mean!" or "I hate when you do X."

The fifteen-year-old may tell you that back then you were much more controlling than you are now. Or he or she may remind you of punishments that were unjust or that your harsh words uttered at the point of exhaustion and morning sickness hurt, nonetheless. He or she may be upset to have been homeschooled, or that the other parent yells so much, or that s/he is unprepared for advanced math.

A 25-year-old may see childhood through a different lens—wondering about the impact of political or religious views on family life, reevaluating the family hierarchy, identifying abuse, and calling out discipline tactics.

It's really tough to listen to your child—the one for whom you'd gladly throw yourself in front of a train—tell you that you failed somehow in your parenting. It's too easy to dismiss the child's viewpoint by saying, "I'm not so strict now" or "That was a long time ago and you know I've changed" or "It doesn't seem to have hurt you any" or even, "You'll understand better when you're a parent."

All of these may be true. But they don't address the central point of the complaint—pain.

When your kids tell you that you were a meaningful constitutive part of their pain, it is your right and responsibility to hear them out and to be open to the possibility that you had a role in creating/fostering/causing it.

It's especially difficult to listen to our children when they are right—when we were too harsh or we permitted the other parent to be cruel. We don't remember the punishments or the emotional outbursts in the way a child does. Children are vulnerable and small (as in, they have small bodies). Their memories will seem disproportionate to what we remember because for us, we operated from a place of power and size, which diminishes the volume and scale of the disciplinary choice.

Think of it like this. Imagine that you are happily walking along on the street, and out of the blue you hear a bullhorn: "Stop walking. This is the police." Without a single additional word, your body will go into what I call "tuning fork" mode. The volume and the authority of the speaker will cause your nervous system to immediately

 Brave Writer

ping into electricity and anxiety. You'll feel in trouble, even if you're not. This is how our kids feel when we yell at them.

When we raise our voices, we put our children's nervous systems on high alert. Naturally. Automatically. We are big and powerful, and they are not. Their memories of those moments will match what happened to their insides, not what we explain with logic and reason on the outside.

When your child inevitably comes to you in pain (I hate writing, this is too hard, you are mean, why won't you listen to me?, I don't agree with X), it is your privilege as the person closest to that child, the one who loves that person more than anyone else on the planet, to simply hear what he or she has to say.

Sometimes it takes all the courage you can screw together to sit on your hands, and zip your lip, and simply listen without recourse or response. It helped me to have a few key phrases I could say when confronted with my children's memories that were unpleasant for me to hear.

"What else...?"

"Can you tell me more about that?"

"How else did you feel?"

"What do you wish had happened?"

"Am I still doing that now in some way?"

"I bet it feels awful to not have the power to make the choices for your own life."

"I regret that too."

"I wish it had been different for you too."

"I'm sorry."

"I'm so sorry."

"I am here if you need to discuss this again or any new thoughts come up."

"Is there anything else you want me to know?"

My parents are divorced. When I was about 30 and in therapy, my mom came to me one time (she, too, was in therapy) and made me the most meaningful promise of my life. This is what she told me.

"Julie, I know there are many ways I failed you as a mother, particularly during the divorce years. As long as I am alive, I want you to know there is no time when you can't come to me to tell me about the pain I caused you during that time. I know there will be new moments where the divorce is painful to you now, as an adult. I am willing to hear you and talk with you about any of it, as long as I'm alive. There is no expiration date on discussing your pain."

I can't tell you the relief it was to hear those words— and I have taken her up on that commitment more than

© Julie (Bogart) Sweeney | bravewriter.com   Brave Writer

once. However, conversely (and ironically) because I know that door is wide open, I don't always need to walk through it. I feel heard and known.

I, too, have caused my children pain. Recently I remember Noah and I discussing a hard season in his childhood. I began to describe it as I remembered it and he said, "Mom, let's not get into revisionist history here. *this* is how it happened."

It stopped me cold. I remembered—he owns his story of what happened to him. My memory will never be as important to him as his is. And because I was not the vulnerable child, I am far more likely to whitewash my role in his pain. So I stopped, and I listened, and I suffered a little.

We all want to be heard. We want our version of our life's events to be acknowledged as real for us. We want someone to say, "You were hurt. I'm so sorry." Our kids want that from us. Give it to them. We enhance the space for connection and love when we do, which is the goal all along anyway, right?

Quote of the day

This is beautiful. It speaks to me of my memories as a child and what I wish would have been offered to me and is a reminder of what I want to give to my children. Thank you so much for articulating this so beautifully Julie.

Sarah Washington

Sustaining thought

If you want to connect deeply and forever with your children all you have to do is listen to them.

Day 43

All About Homeschooling

I've noticed a trend in home education products and services. More and more they resemble the schedule, trappings, and services of school. In fact, I remember a friend saying to me one time that she felt like she lived in her car. She was driving to sports practices, music lessons, a co-op, tutoring for math and science, and her kids were also in an acting company.

Her comment cracked me up: "Wouldn't it be great if all of these services and classes were in one building and happened all day in a row? It would make my life so much easier."

I thought she was joking, but when I saw that she wasn't, I said, "That does exist. It's called school."

Now she cracked up! "You're right! Oh my gosh, you're right. I didn't even think of that! What am I doing?"

That was a good question.

In our desire to give our kids a great education, we routinely slide into the ditch of school expectations. It takes guts and vigilance not to. Usually there are two moments in time that are especially susceptible to this line of thinking: when we begin (sometime in elementary school) and when we "re-up" for high school (that time where we fear it "all counts").

Yet once we get past the hurdle of schoolishness, we usually discover that there are riches in our homeschool lives that could never be duplicated in a school context. It's not that we shouldn't take piano lessons or join sports teams. It's not wrong to use tutors or to join co-ops with their classes and homework.

Rather, we want to aim for a lifestyle that honors the unique values of homeschool too, and not shoehorn our lives into some inferior, cobbled-together version of school.

For instance, when I began Brave Writer, I knew that what I really wanted for myself and our families is an online class program that supported parents as writing coaches and allies to their kids. I didn't simply want to teach writing to kids so parents wouldn't have to. In fact, I felt strongly that parents who wanted to home educate should get the training and support they craved to do that very job!

So we enroll parents with kids in all our foundational courses. This ensures that children will finish a class and wind up with parents who can continue to lead that education with confidence and good partnership writing skills.

We also offer classes that don't require you to keep a specific schedule. Homeschool thrives when you don't have to meet the demands of a busy clock schedule. Why should you have to promise yourself that you will always be home every Tuesday and Thursday at 11:00 a.m. to log in for a live class? What if the art museum has a free exhibit on a Thursday? What if your best friend invites you to a seaside picnic on a Tuesday at noon? Homeschool thrives when you have the freedom to come and go, to pay attention to the moods and energy levels of your family. Our classes give you that freedom to participate when it works best for you—anywhere around the globe in any time zone.

Our products are not systematic schemes with daily schedules that forget about national holidays or the two-week ski vacation you take every January. I believe in "less is more" —less systematic, more immersive, less rigidly scheduled and more open-ended process.

What happens initially is that some Brave Writer parents feel a little at sea. This is not how they envisioned education because they are usually products of traditional schooling. Yet as they wade into our waters, they are liberated—they discover that one principle at a time; one project over several weeks; one process tested, explored, and practiced; does far more to instruct than daily metrics of worksheets or pages read.

The flow of homeschool depends on these principles (and they guide everything we produce and offer at Brave Writer):

- Flexibility to follow the unique rhythms and lifestyles of individual children and families.

- Immersion for short bursts (3-6 week classes, for instance; one writing project per month; one literary element per month; poetry paired with tea once per week).

- Relationship-building instruction. We are as much about fostering a healthy, reciprocal, respectful relationship between child and parent as we are about teaching writing.

- Freedom to take risks. It's important to create a space for failure, missteps, accidents. As we create room for error, we create space also for inspiration, surprise, and breakthroughs.

- Available instruction any time of year. Our classes start and stop all year long, even in the summer months. We know that you aren't always ready to work on writing only in August and January. We also know you can't be expected to keep working on one thing every week of the year or semester. Homeschool just isn't like that. Having many chances to jump into helpful writing instruction gives you the freedom to wait for the right moment for each child—joining us when it is best for you, not shoe-horning us into your life against your child's better interest.

- Variety! School gives us Composition 1, 2, and 3. Brave Writer gives us Nature Journaling, Movie

 © Julie (Bogart) Sweeney | bravewriter.com Brave Writer

Discussion Clubs, Photography and Writing, Poetry, Grammar Workshops, Fan Fiction, and so much more. Writing across the curriculum is a sterile way to say: Writing in all kinds of natural, inspiring contexts.

Feel free to homeschool your children. Follow the unique rhythms and currents of your family's learning style. Tailor make your lives to suit you, not some gray-scale version of school in a building.

You get to have a home that creates the environment for learning to pop through all of your daily interactions. Do it! Feel free. Brave Writer is here to help and to honor those impulses that live inside you. That's because I homeschooled too. I remember what worked and what didn't work.

Quote of the day

I love you, Julie. It's a reminder to not value the tool over the connection. I want to be connected with my kids. It's probably the deepest reason for homeschooling.

Melanie Levy

Sustaining thought

Your homeschool is a reflection of who you are, not how schools operate. Lean into it.

Day 44

Startle Your Kids!

One way to bring energy into your family life is for you, the homeschooling parent, to embark on your own adventure. Pick an adventure that is yours alone (not bound to your kids in any way). That adventure can be grand (like planning a trip to Europe by yourself—I mean it!) or it can be homespun (like refurbishing dolls or growing organic vegetables in your front yard).

We want our kids to pursue their interests with commitment and heart. We certainly homeschool them with that energy (after all, home education is *our* grand adventure—truly). Yet because the homeschool adventure is bound up in them, it is somewhat invisible to them (they don't realize it is an adventure for you), unlike, say, learning to surf, or painting with oils, or writing a novel in a month, or going back to grad school, or running a half marathon, or horseback riding in Montana, or getting your real estate license.

Take it in baby steps. Perhaps you will simply take yourself to an art museum sans children for the sake of pure pleasure. I did that once. I met a friend from the Internet (we had not yet met in person) in Chicago to go to the Art Institute together over a weekend. It was a

 © Julie (Bogart) Sweeney | bravewriter.com Brave Writer

rare escape and it took me some time to save the money for the flight. That commitment to art, though, carried me and my kids a long way in our homeschool. It was a natural part of our lives because it had become a passion of mine—one I nurtured without them around all the time.

You might start running each day—short half-mile lengths, alternating with walks, until you build up to a 10K or a half marathon. Your kids will then say about you, "Yeah, my mom's a runner." It will mean something to them— the commitment, the willingness to make time for it, the sheer joy at having achieved your goal. It's a meta-lesson in learning and passion, determination and practice. They get to root for you and celebrate your achievements—a lesson in valuing you, the way you value them.

I have a friend who has a dream book. In it, she puts pictures of her aspirations for different years of her life. As we paged through it together one time, I noticed that she had a photo of a trip to learn to surf in Mexico. She had taken that trip in time for her 50th birthday. I looked at that beautiful blue image. I grew up next to the ocean yet had never learned to surf. I made that my goal for my 50th birthday...and went! She surprised me and met me there. It was a magical week, one I'll never forget.

Of course, when my kids were younger, my adventures were on a smaller, less expensive, scale. I learned to quilt, I wrote articles for magazines, I got interested in birding, I became passionate about Shakespeare, poetry, and art, and I took guitar lessons.

Each time you branch out for yourself, you are investing in your family. It sounds counterintuitive, but it's the truth. Because you are such a zealot for home-everythingness, I trust you to not overdo it (you won't let yourself!). Rather, what I'm suggesting is that you not let your own adult life—these healthy years—scroll by in service exclusively of your children, thinking that a later date will come when you can go to grad school or visit a full service spa in the Red Rocks of Arizona.

You grew up to this age so that you could use your full adult powers for good—for your family, for your community, and also, just as importantly, for yourself. When you take that time and initiative to create a good happy life for yourself, as much as you do for your kids, you give your family energy—energy that rebounds into home education. The world becomes alive with possibility for all of you.

Most importantly, your kids can look ahead to adulthood and *see* that it is worth growing up and learning all kinds of things because that's when you get to *do cool stuff*! Like Mom! Like Dad!

Startle your children! Be the model of adulthood to which you hope they aspire.

Last thing: If you find yourself frustrated that your kids aren't into learning as much as you are, forget them for a bit. Dive deep. Learn all you want. The more you indulge your cravings, rather than foisting them on your

 Brave Writer

kids, the more likely it is they will want to "get involved" eventually, in some aspect of your current passion. Passion is contagious.

Surprise your family; surprise yourself! Set a goal today and go after it, right in the middle of all the muddle. Post your ideas (and what you are already doing) below to inspire us. I'd love photos, if you have them.

Quote of the day

> I'm doing a health challenge and getting out walking more. Also, finally painting a canvas for our master bedroom.
>
> *Amanda Jensen*

Sustaining thought

Be the adult you want to be; go on an adult-sized adventure and make your kids proud of you!

Day 45

Stick Up for Yourself Inside

Fifteen years ago, I started an online discussion board called The Trapdoor Society, mostly for homeschool mom friends. The concept was this. Because our days were filled with small children and home-keeping demands, we needed an escape—a trapdoor through which we could pursue our self-education: art, literature, film, politics, religion, poetry, and more. We'd be friendly and supportive when we disagreed and we'd help each other expand our worlds together.

In other words, Internet Utopia.

In other words, good luck with that.

We did become incredible friends. There are still about 40 of us in touch today. But those friendships also survived some truly painful clashes of personality, belief systems, emotional meltdowns, and even a version of trolling, though that word didn't exist back then.

I remember spending hours crafting response posts in my head when I felt maligned or judged or misunderstood. Years later, I noticed a cartoon that expressed my feelings perfectly. "Someone is wrong on the Internet."

© Julie (Bogart) Sweeney | bravewriter.com Brave Writer

Underneath that surface reason, though, was another one that was invisible to me at the time. Fear. I didn't want to be wrong. I didn't want to be misunderstood. I didn't want to have made an irrevocable choice.

When criticism came my way, I wanted to fight back— at least on the outside. If I could get everyone out there to agree that I was okay, then I would finally allow myself to feel okay inside.

The benefit of aging is the increasing awareness that it is nigh to impossible to get all the people out there to agree that you are perfectly wonderful as you are. (I know, I've tried.)

No one likes you enough to do that for you. They're all too busy trying to get you to tell them that they're okay as they are.

One of the reasons it's tough to hear our kids tell us that some of our choices were painful to them is that we especially want their approval—after all, we are "sacrificing" careers, manicures, a good tennis game, grad school, hobbies, and beautifully decorated homes to ensure they have the best possible childhoods. How they can't know that, can't see that, can't forgive us for our foibles is incomprehensible.

The only way out is inner confidence—to firm up your shaky insides with your resilient belief that you are conscientious, intentional, and sincere. These three qualities won't prevent mistakes or the possibility that you may overreach. They won't guarantee romanticized notions of success. But they can be the firm base from which you continue to grow, revise, and expand your life's vision.

If you resist the temptation to defend yourself to others, but instead, take any criticism or disagreement as a chance to revisit your personal creed and practice, you will slowly but surely see that you are, in fact, that worthwhile person you wish others could see. You'll know it from the inside—that your choices and your vision are perfectly valid for you.

Meanwhile, rather than eviscerate your persecutors with better arguments or lengthy diatribes, go soft on the outside. The old proverb, "A gentle word turns away wrath" may not always work in intimate relationships, but it does provide a neat exit online.

It is often the perfect response to children—respond in the opposite spirit. They come with anger and force, you respond with internal strength and gentle words: "I hear you. That sounds awful. I want better for you."

Strong on the inside, soft on the outside.

Respond in the opposite spirit.

Stick up for yourself to yourself.

Trust—you don't know the outcome of this grand risky experiment. Take it one day at a time, with your conscientiousness, sincerity, and intentionality to guide you.

Quote of the day

With realization of one's own potential and self-confidence in one's ability, one can build a better world.

Dalai Lama

Sustaining thought

As you begin to know and understand yourself, others will know and understand you too.

Day 46

Is it Confusing?

Is it difficult? Are you worried?

Good. Means you're doing it right. Means you want to do it right. Means you're evaluating and considering, caring and revising.

How can you possibly find the right program and not ever reconsider?

How can you teach high school math when you found it impossible yourself?

Why wouldn't you worry about your socially awkward tween or your dyslexic 2nd grader or your moody 16-year-old?

Of course you're tired—anxious, weary, feeling alone.

You have assigned yourself an enormous task—the complete education of your precious children, without having done any training, without any certainty that you can do it. You live in a petrie dish of your own making— hoping that if you bring together the right ingredients with your children, an educated person will emerge and contribute to the world.

© Julie (Bogart) Sweeney | bravewriter.com Brave Writer

Even more—there are no guarantees your children will thank you for the herculean effort you are making on their behalf. They may grow up, go to college, marry, and say, "Heck no! I'm putting my own kids in school." What then? Will that feel like you somehow failed them?

So, yes. You worry. Some days you feel overwhelmed and sad—wondering if this is how homeschool is supposed to feel. You want joy, natural learning, enthusiasm to explore the wide open world. You hope to see ties form between bickering children, and you want to feel close to your teens as they move away from you into their inevitable independence.

Will you do a good enough job? Will your kids agree?

Yes, this is how it is supposed to feel. Lean into it. As long as you homeschool, some doubt will ride sidecar to all the good you do every day. Not every decision will pan out, not every day will show fruit, not every effort will be worthwhile.

Yet if you stick with it, if you make adjustments that are considerate of your children as they are (as they show themselves to you), over time (cumulatively), your children *will* receive an education that suits them to adult life.

Doubt, worry, confusion, anxiety—as long as these are not swamping you (preventing you from doing the work of home education), they are simply conditions that go with the territory.

Keep going. Keep trying. Keep expanding your options.

Once in a while pause—admire how far you've come, how many things you've learned, how much you know now about education that you didn't know when you started. Remind yourself that you are still learning and will know even more in another year! How grand is that!?

You're okay now. Just as you are. Breathe.

Quote of the day

> *The only difference between the families who seem to have it all together and those who seem to have a lot of struggles is honesty. Found this out over the years, when the seemingly perfect homeschooling families facades crumbled as they inevitably do.*
>
> *Emma Hamilton*

Sustaining thought

Doubt and worry are characteristics of conscientious parents. Keep going—your confusion will clear as you patiently apply what you learn one day at a time.

 Brave Writer

Day 47

Single Efforts Can Teach Profound Skills

Because we focus on depth and connection when we teach, we don't need repetition of activities to the degree that schools need it. We aren't pushing kids through material to ensure we don't "miss anything." On the contrary, we have the opportunity to patiently focus on an individual moment in time, looking at a specific skill, working with that child until it is understood.

It may be that you will revise a single piece of writing with one child this year. If you do a thorough, caring, patient job with your child, ensuring that the child feels connected to you and open to the teaching (through kindness, consideration, and helpfulness), that single editing/revision experience may be enough for the entire year! It is possible to learn it all in that one paper—enough for this year's effort. When a child is well taught—when you care to give full commitment once in a while to a specific skill—your student will "get it" and not need repeated pushes and nudges and practice over and over again to the point of irritation and tedium.

Instead, your child will be able to take what you imparted and then practice as needed using the skills acquired in that one event.

Likewise, you might find that your child produced one fabulous session of copywork where the handwriting looked elegant, and the proportions on the page were spot on, and the care to copy punctuation and indentation succeeded. That experience teaches so much more than dozens of pages of half-hearted effort.

We focus too much on what isn't getting done instead of recognizing the power of specific, intentional, well-executed moments in time. Do your kids need to love every lesson? No. They don't have to fall in love with writing to become good writers. They need the skills—they can get them with far less pain if you change your expectations. Quality instruction, affection and closeness over quantity of products.

Trust these single efforts. They are working better for you than you know.

Quote of the day

I'm so grateful for your posts! It's so hard to resist comparing my kids' progress and output to what schooled kids do, even though I know it's a comparison that is ludicrous beyond measure. Thank you for yet another perfectly timed reminder!

Julia Swancy

© Julie (Bogart) Sweeney | bravewriter.com Brave Writer

Sustaining thought

Intentional, invested, infrequent lessons do more to teach than tedious repetition.

Day 48

You Have Time to Prepare

Do you remember how to divide fractions? I didn't. I had a 4th grade math book whose page I turned and discovered, "Oops! We are up to division of fractions. I can't remember how to do that."

I whisked myself away to the garage to teach myself. My kids made messes in the living room.

I returned ready to show Noah how to divide fractions. He performed the task easily. At the end of the page, he commented, "So I don't have to really remember this? I won't need fractions as an adult? I only need to know them for today, right?"

Ha! He took a different lesson than the one I meant to impart. My inability to remember how to divide fractions stood out, naked and then ashamed. I countered that my handicaps in math were just that—skills I didn't get to use when I needed them. I hoped for better for him, and I told him that I would do a better job of preparing to be his teacher in the future.

It's with this experience in mind that I make the following recommendation. It is wise to prepare. In fact,

 Brave Writer

it is essential to learn how to home educate your kids. It is entirely on task to read blogs, Facebook groups, books, and the directions that precede any lesson you expect your kids to complete.

In fact, it is so on task, may I make a bold statement? I know you don't have time to study "learning" by yourself, in some ideal context of private, quiet, peaceful hours in the day. I know this.

So, here's my advice: just do it—right in the middle of the day with kids all around you, "off-task" in dress up clothes, acting out *Frozen* one more time. Tuck your feet under you, snuggle up to the corner of the sectional, and read, scroll, page. Use headphones if you need to. Highlighter in hand, read. Take notes. Absorb.

It is so much better to let go of today's and tomorrow's lessons in order to drill down to the essential ingredients of math or writing, or to understand a period in history, or to get a glimpse of how the science experiment should go and what its objective is, than to muddle forward with doubt and your child's resistance.

It is not better to just "get it done" and hope for the best. There is no "automatic" method for any learning. It just doesn't happen that way. Depth, immersion, exploration, and guidance are the core values of education.

We are concerned with completion of pages or curricula, and then we worry that our kids aren't making progress, and we hope for a quick fix—some solution that won't require us to take valuable time to understand before implementation.

But this approach is backwards. You didn't go to college (most of you) to get a teaching credential. You're becoming educators on the fly (even unschoolers are embarking on a huge new project of how to be that parent who facilitates learning or invests deeply in a child's passions). These choices necessitate information that informs *how* you spend time with your kids, and *what* you impart.

You will feel so much better if you have a handle on the contours of a subject area, than if you plod through a book hoping for magic (that the lesson leaps from the page without you knowing why or how it works).

You do have time. For all the hours you don't spend in preparation, you will find yourself frustrated with basic problems. Why isn't my child of 10 spelling well? This is answered quickly in a book that explains the natural stages of growth in writing. Ten-year-olds don't spell well. Here's why, here's how to foster the continued growth.

Without that bit of knowledge, you will be tempted to push your child or to shame him for not spelling well. I know. I've done all of that. I've pushed, I've shamed, I've blamed, I've plowed forward in a curriculum expecting it to teach and finding out it did not.

Then a new day dawned. I saw that my home life was fluid—we didn't have set school hours, we didn't

 Brave Writer

have a teacher's lounge for me. We had the mixed up mess of living and learning and all my insecurities about parenting and educating—together in one living room, at one kitchen table. It finally occurred to me: If I was unsure about how to impart a specific skill set for them or share about an area of passion for me, I could spend daytime looking into it. Right when I wanted to.

I wanted my kids to have an art education, but had no idea how to go about it. We spent time in the library where they read books they wanted, and I checked out books about art. I read them. I bought some. I started hanging prints on the wall. Finally, I ordered the six video set of *Sister Wendy's Story of Painting*. I put them on every day for a couple of weeks, right after breakfast. My kids were free to come and go, but I took notes. They remember this period of our homeschool.

The foundation from that season was laid *in me*. I couldn't wait to go to museums with the kids. They were excited to see paintings we'd already viewed in the video series.

I didn't set out to make this a lesson for them. It was a lesson for me. I didn't "go to another room" to understand it and then come back with the pretense of "Aha! Here's the lesson you have to learn now." Rather, I learned, in front of them.

Did our Sister Wendy odyssey take time away from math? Yes, yes it did.

It also showed me the value of taking time to prepare the feast of ideas I hoped would be my children's education.

The benefits were life-changing:

- to understand—to be prepared
- to get behind the lessons to *why* the lessons
- to discover the germ of value in the material
- to grow as an educator
- to fuel my creativity
- to spark my enthusiasm
- to feel competent.
- to hold realistic expectations for each age and subject area

These are the benefits of preparation. You deserve these benefits. Take the time to get them.

Quote of the day

Yes! And as I start hole-punching Writer's Jungle this morning and then sat in the dining room highlighting, all children stopped by to see what I was up to...what a tremendous model we provide when we are absorbed in something true. Great post!

Heather Weller

© Julie (Bogart) Sweeney | bravewriter.com   Brave Writer

Sustaining thought

You deserve to benefit from time spent preparing—so take the time to do it.

Day 49

Today is a Gift

I know you know. I know everyone keeps telling you that.

Yet it's true. Heartbreakingly so.

Family members living with cancer, random bullets shot at optimistic college students in Santa Barbara, martial law in Bangkok, a missing 22-year-old in Cincinnati, never-planned car accidents, aging parents losing their words and memories, births with unexpected complications.

The assault on living by the dangerous and dying is relentless. The best we can do is to make cakes for birthday parties, have friends stop by to grill on holiday weekends, root for our teams in the playoffs, stand in the sunshine and feel its warmth, today.

I spent yesterday decluttering more than a decade's worth of stuff bought with real dollars earned through hard work that brought various levels of comfort, pleasure, and distraction. Twenty bags destined for the trash.

Nothing lasts, no matter how precious.

Today's a good day to let go of a grudge, to eat ice cream, to sit a little longer with the needy child, to not

 © Julie (Bogart) Sweeney | bravewriter.com Brave Writer

take "it" personally, to reach out to the far away suffering person, to share a meaningful memory with the person closest to you.

Homeschooling is one way to wander through the years—a rich, layered, intimate way.

I don't like it when people tell me to be grateful or urge me to be happy on days when I'm on the verge of tears.

Occasionally, though, when I'm going through the motions, it's good to remember the bargain we've all made in life—there is no promised length to our days. Today is it.

So if you are in that place today—doing the routine without much thought, I hope you find a pocket of time to pause and remember. It's Memorial Day weekend in the US. Remember the ones who died and have afforded us this life, remember the ones who are yet alive and love you.

May today be a good day in the string of days that are your life.

Quote of the day

Just what I needed, Julie. Life seems unsympathetically relentless at the moment, but there are always beautiful things if we take a moment and look up.

Elisa Leidenheimer Cottrell

Sustaining thought

This day is all we can be sure of—and it is the best of days—no matter what.

Day 50

Five Magic Words

Get a dose of at least one of these per day and see if your home environment doesn't improve. I've provided two possible examples of each one to get your creative juices going. Build from these! Check out another great suggestion from a Brave Writer mom in the Quote of the Day.

1. Surprise

- A margin note in the math book

- Cake for breakfast

2. Chance

- Roll of the dice—numbers represent "how many" of whatever work for the day (number of math problems, number of letters traced, number of pages or sentences or words read...)

- Flip a coin—Heads means working independently for ten minutes; tails means working with a partner for ten minutes (child chooses which subject for independence or partnership)

3. Mystery

- Handwritten clues leading to a new board game or snack or treat

- Use invisible ink to reveal new copywork or dictation passage

4. Secret

- Provide a lock-'n-key diary for secret entries

- Tell a child a secret plan to spend time with them (that day, later in the week...)

5. Discover

- Walk, bike, kayak somewhere new

- Explore little-known works of authors or poets you love

Good luck!

Quote of the day

Great ideas! Thanks for sharing. I can't wait to try them out. Our chance: we write out everything we have to do for the day – math, reading, snack, history, chore, free play (whatever happens to be on the agenda) – each on a separate piece of paper, fold 'em up, drop in a bag/jar/bowl, and then take turns picking what we do next! It's especially fun when we pick snack right after breakfast and then free play right after that! My kids love the suspense!

Lisa Blough

© Julie (Bogart) Sweeney | bravewriter.com   Brave Writer

Sustaining thought

Bring the sparkle back into your homeschool through surprise, chance, mystery, secrets, and discovery.

Brave Writer

New To Brave Writer?

The principles you've enjoyed in this volume are the ones I use to help you teach writing!

The best tool to transform your writing life is *The Writer's Jungle*. *The Writer's Jungle* is the centerpiece to the Brave Writer lifestyle. In it, homeschooling parents find the insight, support and tools that help them become the most effective writing coaches their children will ever have.

The missing ingredient in writing curricula isn't how to structure a paragraph (information that can be readily found on the Internet). You don't need more facts about topic sentences or how to use libraries. Grammar and spelling are not the key components in writing, either, much to the chagrin of some English teachers.

- Are you tired of the blank page blank stare syndrome (hand a child a blank page; get back a blank stare)?

- Are you worried that you aren't a good enough writer to teach writing?

- Is your child bright, curious, and verbal but seems to lose her words when she is asked to write?

- Do you wonder how to expand the ideas in the sentences your child writes without damaging your relationship?

- Has writing become a place where tears flow and fears surface?

- Is your child a prolific writer and you aren't sure how to direct him to the next level?

- Have you tried "just about everything" and feel ready to give up on writing?

If you answered 'yes' to any of these questions, then *The Writer's Jungle* is for you! Purchase it today.

If you aren't quite ready to make the big investment, get your feet wet with an issue of The Arrow (3rd – 6th grades) or The Boomerang (7th – 10th grades)—intended to help you teach the mechanics of writing naturally and painlessly!

Enjoy your journey to Brave Writing!